THE LOST FILMS FANZINE #5 SPRING 2021

Joe Manganiello's new look as Deathstroke in Snyder's version of JUSTICE LEAGUE © 2021
Warner Bros/DC Comics

who loses everything overnight. "I was very excited for it," Manganiello concluded.

Not only that, Manganiello also wrote up his own proposed Deathstroke film that unfortunately died along with the original *The Batman*. "I worked with an Oscar-nominated writer on that treatment, and it was one of those projects that got canceled during that period. There were maybe seven different Deathstroke projects that all didn't happen over the course of four years. It's one of those funny things in Hollywood and in life where you've just got to let it go." Though it's no consolation for getting booted out of *The Batman*, Manganiello will at least get to reprise Deathstroke in the Snyder Cut of *Justice League* in newly filmed footage.

UNMADE SNYDER COMICBOOK In yet another piece of unmade news relating to the DCEU, Zach Snyder pitched a prequel comic book to DC that would have explained how and why the Joker killed Robin prior to the events of *Batman v Superman: Dawn of Justice*.

Snyder told the YouTube channel SnyderCutBR that, "You know, we talked about doing a, I guess it would be DC, they decided not to do it. But we did talk about doing a mini-kind of comic book run on the death of Robin, right? And what happened? How Joker killed Robin and what it did to Batman and started him down this dark, darker road that ended, kind of culminated, with the arrival of Superman."

UNMADE MARVEL And now for a much older aborted comic book movie: During a Wizard World panel, Michael E. Uslan, who produced *Batman* (1989), revealed that after that film's success, he pitched a *Luke Cage* movie to Universal and Motown Productions. "Right after our first *Batman* movie, I optioned the rights from Marvel to *Luke Cage, Hero for Hire*," Uslan said during the panel. "This was when Marvel was mired. All they had was Captain America, and Fantastic Four, neither of which could be released theatrically. Marvel was in a mess." (Uslan is speaking to the unsuccesful film adaptations of those properties.) Uslan explained that Cage/Power Man was a good place to start because it wouldn't be as complicated to film (as opposed to a flying hero like say, Green Lantern or Thor). Despite being pitched after the '89 *Batman*, Uslan envisioned the film taking place on the streets of New York in either the late 1970s or early 1980s. Sadly, Motown Films folded shortly after, and Universal was sold off to a

3

A MUPPET CHRISTMAS CAROL © 1992 Walt Disney LUKE CAGE © Marvel Comics/Disney

new company. That double-whammy effectively ended the efforts to bring Luke Cage to the big screen. In 2016, a *Luke Cage* series did at least premiere on Netflix, and sadly ended on an unresolved cliffhanger as did Netflix's other Marvel shows.

IRON FIST SEASON 3 PLANS And for more current unmade Marvel news, *Iron Fist* star Finn Jones revealed what the plans were for the third season had it not been cancelled. Just for a refresher, Season 2 ended with Colleen Wing inheriting Danny's Iron Fist power, while Danny departed for Asia. "Raven [Metzner], who was the showrunner for the second season, and I were sure that there was gonna be a season 3," said Jones. "So we had already devised the whole thing. I was so excited to get into that. It really was gonna be about Danny finally assuming the role of the Iron Fist, fully accomplished, fully charged up, and fully in control of his shit, as well. It was gonna be this amazing story [with] Danny and Ward off in foreign lands as a buddy storyline almost. And then, you had Colleen in New York, isolated with this new power, struggling to come to terms with her identity and with this power. At some point, we would have met again and probably formed this crazy power couple [or] superhero relationship."

MISSING MUPPET SONG FOUND Last year, just in time for Christmas, a long lost song from *The Muppet Christmas Carol* was found. The song, "When Love Is Gone", was originally placed in the film during a scene where Scrooge's fiancée, Belle, sings it to him. Disney removed it because they felt it wouldn't appeal to younger audiences. (To be thorough, it was cut from the theatrical version, reinstated for the VHS release, and then lost again for the DVD release!) When working on a 4K remaster of the film, the lost reel with the song was found.

"I was so excited," director Brian Henson told BBC Radio 2 about the discovery. "They actually hid it... so I went down and they said: 'But before we show it to you, we've got something else we want to show you'. And they put up reel four of *Christmas Carol* with When Love Is Gone." It was with great reluctance that Henson allowed the song to be cut, so he is quite happy to finally see it reinstated.

THE LOST FILMS FANZINE

FEATURES

CHARLIE GEMORA'S LOST FILMS He was the greatest ape-suit performer of all time, and also the creator of some amazing lost projects...**5**

SUPERMAN REBORN Trevor Snyder examines one of the more ambitious unborn Superman movies...**18**

MIKADO ZOMBIE Matthew Lamont reveals the original plan for the film, which changed due to a string of horrific murders...**31**

WAR OF THE WORLDS THAT WEREN'T PART III Stan Hyde concludes his cinematic journey through WotW adaptations that didn't happen...**33**

LEE POWERS REVIEWS ANAK NG BULKAN '97...**40**

TEENAGE MUTANT NINJA TURTLES IV Between 1994-97 was developed a truly wild, unmade TMNT sequel...**42**

KING GHIDORAH FLIES SOLO Get the rundown on Toho's axed King Ghidorah spin-off from 1999...**48**

LIVE ACTION PEANUTS? Matthew Lamont remembers NBC's Big Stuffed Dog...**50**

GRIZZLY II: REVENGE! It's finally here, the editor reviews the long lost sequel...**54**

BLU-RAY REVIEWS...**61**

LOST LETTERS...**62**

THE LOST FILMS FANZINE, VOL. 2, #5 SPRING 2021

EDITOR AND PUBLISHER: JOHN LEMAY. SPECIAL CONSULTANT: KYLE BYRD. SPECIAL THANKS THIS ISSUE TO TREVOR SNYDER, STAN HYDE, LEE POWERS AND MATTHEW LAMONT.

THE LOST FILMS FANZINE IS PUBLISHED FOUR TIMES A YEAR. THE COPY-RIGHTS AND TRADEMARKS OF THE IMAGES FEATURED THEREIN ARE HELD BY THEIR RESPECTIVE OWNERS. THE LOST FILMS FANZINE ACKNOWLEDGES THE RIGHTS OF THE CREATORS AND THE COPYRIGHT HOLDERS OF THE IMAGES THEREIN AND DOES NOT SEEK TO INFRINGE UPON THOSE RIGHTS. PHOTO-GRAPHS AND POSTERS ARE REPRODUCED IN THE SPIRIT OF PUBLICITY. ALL TEXT COPYRIGHT THE RESPECTIVE AUTHORS OF THE ARTICLES. CONTACT THE EDITOR @ JPLEMAY@PLATEAUTEL.NET

A year ago, I not only created *The Lost Films Fanzine* out of quarantine-induced boredom, but also the desire to provide quick/cheap entertainment to fellow cinephiles with obscure tastes like myself who were also bored, cooped up, and looking for something to read. Like so many others, I also needed a distraction from a gloomy year. What has pleased me more than anything else is the responses I've gotten to the 'zine, not via Amazon reviews, but personal Facebook Messages from people who told me what a nice distraction both the 'zine and the Facebook page have been over the past year. So, to anyone who's written to me over Facebook I just wanted to say thank you, it means a lot and just shows that we're all in this together!

As the 'zine progresses into its second year, I'm pleased to see it continue it's eclectic mix of content. (Did you ever think you'd find a 'zine with articles on an unmade fourth *Teenage Mutant Ninja Turtles* movie and the lost films of ape suit performer Charles Gemora?) I'm also pleased that I'm getting more regular contributors to join Stan Hyde and his Theatre of What Should Have Been series. This issue, I'm happy to bring in two new writers: Trevor Snyder and Matthew Lamont. Trevor is endeavoring to uncover the truth of the many unmade comic book movies in his Snyder's Superhero Corner (my corny name for it, don't blame him) while Matthew, on the other hand, runs wild with eclectic subjects like J-horror and long forgotten NBC children's specials. If that's not eclectic, then I don't know what is! So, here's to another great year...well, a great year for the 'zine at least!

John LeMay, March 2021

NEWS

Jared Leto as the Joker in new footage from JUSTICE LEAGUE's Snyder Cut. © 2021 Warner Bros/DC Comics

As the release of the *Justice League* Snyder Cut comes nearer (actually, by the time you read this it will be out) there's been a deluge of news on unmade DC movies. Joe Manganiello, who appeared as Deathstroke in *Justice League's* theatrical post-credits scene, recalled that when he shot the scene with Snyder, the dialogue between he and Lex Luthor (Jesse Eisenberg) was meant to set up the events of *The Batman*.

But, plans changed, and so the post-credits scene had to be altered. "They reshot all of Jesse's dialogue to tease *Justice League Part 2*, which was going to be about the Injustice League," Manganiello explained. Notice that Manganiello said "was" instead of is, which means plans for a second *Justice League* have already changed yet again! In terms of relating to *The Batman*, Manganiello said, "All of that dialogue [between Deathstroke and Lex Luthor] was about Batman originally, and it was changed to lines like 'Shouldn't we have a league of our own?'"

Originally, *The Batman* was to be written and directed by Ben Affleck, who would naturally also reprise his role as Bruce Wayne. As of now, *The Batman* is a totally different film starring Robert Pattinson set to release a year from now. Thanks to Manganiello during an interview with Yahoo Entertainment for his new film, *Archenemy*, a great deal of information on the original *Batman* was just divulged.

"It was a really dark story in which Deathstroke was like a shark or a horror movie villain that was dismantling Bruce's life from the inside out. It was this systemic thing: He killed everyone close to Bruce and destroyed his life to try and make him suffer because he felt that Bruce was responsible for something that happened to him," Manganiello said of the story. (This is also similar to the Season 2 story arc of DC's live action *Titans* series, currently on HBO Max.) Manganiello also compared the story to *The Game* (1997), a David Fincher film about a banker

THE LOST FILMS FANZINE #5 SPRING 2021

THE LOST FILMS OF CHARLES GEMORA

If you're just a run of the mill cinephile, then the name Charles Gemora may not ring a bell. But, if you're a gorilla movie enthusiast, chances are you'll know exactly who I'm talking about, because long before Rick Baker, Gemora was the undisputed king of men in ape suits. While most movie databases credit Gemora with work on one hundred films, his daughter Diana says it was more likely 1,000! That's obviously a lot of films, but this being The Lost Films Fanzine, instead of talking about the films he did make, we'll mostly be talking about the ones that he didn't. But first, some history..

5

Ad for THE GORILLA (1927).

Charles Gemora was born in the Philippines in 1903. When he was a young man, he stowed away on an American freighter to get to Southern California, where he arrived right in the middle of the silent movie boom. He got his foot in the door at Hollywood by doing portraits outside the Universal lot, and someone from the art department hired him. (He had also been one of the extras in the 1923 *Hunchback of Notre Dame*.) Gemora's artistic skills led to him making sculptures for film sets in the 1920s, and this included the legendary *Phantom of the Opera* (1925).

One fateful day he was instructed to make an ape suit for another legendary silent film: *The Lost World* (1925). Though he didn't play the ape man in that film, he got to thinking that with his short stature and talents as a mime, he might as well play the apes too. His next ape suit was for the lost 1927 film *The Gorilla*. The movie is literally about a man in an ape suit committing murders. It was likely inspired in part by Edgar Allen Poe's *Murders in the Rue Morgue*, but the film was for certain based upon a play by Ralph Spence. The movie was shot silent, as talking pictures were still uncommon. (The first, called *The Jazz Singer*, was released that same year.) The movie starred Charles Murray, Fred Kelsey, and Walter Pidgeon. *The Gorilla* would be remade not once, but twice in 1930 and 1939 (today, only the 1939 version survives).

As for Gemora, he was only asked

THE LOST FILMS FANZINE #5 SPRING 2021

Still from THE LEOPARD LADY (1928) with Gemora terrorizing Jacqueline Logan.

to make the head piece on *The Gorilla* but then ended up making the whole suit. When Gemora saw the finished product he was "disgusted" by the suit actor's performance as it was in no way authentic. In the next film he worked on, *The Leopard Lady* (1928), he did play the ape in question. He got the job thanks to *Phantom of the Opera* director Rupert Julian, who also directed this film. *The Leopard Lady* concerned an animal trainer named Paula (the titular Leopard Lady, played by Jacqueline Logan) who goes undercover at a circus. Recently, a number of mysterious murders have occurred-each quite horrific in nature. The culprit, in *Rue Morgue* fashion, turns out to be a gorilla (Gemora). The fly in the ointment turns out to be that the ape is owned and trained by Caesar (Alan Hale), a Cossack who once saved Paula's life. However, when the ape nearly kills her fiancé (*King Kong's* future Carl Denham, Robert Armstrong), she turns him in and has him arrested. The story was based on a play by Edward Childs Carpenter. It was released on January 22, 1928, with a running time of 70 minutes. Today it is lost and was likely one of the films used to set fires for *Gone with the Wind's* fire scenes as film reels were easily flammable!

Gemora next played an ape in *Tarzan the Mighty* (1928), which originally started out with a different Tarzan: Joe Bonomo (he was re-

7

placed by Frank Merrill due to an injury). Gemora played another ape in *Tarzan, the Tiger* (1929). Next up he was Zozo in *The Circus Kid* (1928), followed by performances in *Do Gentlemen Snore*, *Why Do Gorillas Leave Home*, and *His Baby Daze*.

His next performance in 1930's *Ingagi* is renowned for several reasons. For starters, the film has been banned for the last 90 years for reasons I'll get to later. Aside from that notoriety, *Ingagi* is notable for helping to pave the way for *King Kong*, as it features an ape abducting women in the jungle. *Ingagi* is today described by many as a "pre-Code mockumentary exploitation film." They say mockumentary because it's not a real documentary, though it was passed off as one to audiences in 1930. Notably, Gemora's performance in the gorilla suit actually fooled the general audience and experts alike! Needless to say, this was a huge testament to his career.

Actually, Gemora being passed off as a real gorilla is where the trouble began. And, what exactly was wrong with Gemora's gorilla? Well, that necessitates describing the story, which purports to show the real expedition of "Sir Hubert Winstead" of London. Winstead is in the Belgian Congo (filmed outside of Los Angeles) where he finds a tribe of gorilla-worshiping women. Said native women (actresses from America) are given over to gorillas for uh, purposes we won't clarify, but you can fill in the blanks. That's the reason the film drew the ire of censors later on when the Hays Code was established. In fact, in later years, the three prints owned by the Library of Congress were not made available to the general public. Only recently in 2021 did it receive its first ever home video release through Kino Lorber! (See the review later in this issue.)

But, back to 1930, *Ingagi* was a huge hit. Supposedly the film put RKO back in the red when it was shown in their theaters. It also supposedly helped inspire them to greenlight *King Kong* a few years later.

Next up for Gemora was a remake of *The Gorilla*, in which Gemora did play a gorilla this time. However, like the 1927 version, the full film is lost. Today all that remains is Gemora's test footage as the ape, some of which shows him rampaging through a city three years before

Above: RKO theater display for INGAGI. Top Right: Still from INGAGI depicting Gemora's gorilla.

BANNED UNANIMOUSLY." Well, that cut of the film was banned anyways. Obviously it was trimmed in some way so that it could pass muster. Supposedly, the original cut ran 75 minutes, but most sources concur it likely wasn't that long. Nor was the film a huge hit as hoped, but it didn't slow Gemora's momentum one bit.

Shortly after this, Gemora's manager wanted him to fight a real gorilla! A newspaper touted that: "A boxer and a gorilla named Charles II will clash in a novelty bout arranged by Si Masters. The gorilla will be brought into the ring under heavy guard." Thankfully the event never came to pass.

King Kong! The ape roles continued rolling in, and Gemora was next slated to appear in a movie called *The Gorilla Walks*, which turned into *Scared Stiff* (1931). Next was the Bela Lugosi led *Murders in the Rue Morgue* from 1932, which required the censoring of some of Gemora's scenes:

"THE FILM DEALS WITH CERTAIN PERVERSE TESTS ON THE PART OF A MYSTERIOUS INDIVIDUAL WHO WANTS TO CULTIVATE A GORILLA BY MEANS OF HUMAN BLOOD," wrote the Hays Code, which concluded, "ON GROUNDS OF THE AFORESAID THE PICTURE WAS

Like *Rue Morgue*, Gemora's next gorilla project would again see many cuts. The film was *The Sign of the Cross*, which had a notable scene of a gorilla approaching a naked woman tied to a post (again this was all pre-*King Kong* still!). This scene was in the original release, but was cut from the 1938 re-release (it was

9

Several production stills from THE LOST ISLAND (1934).

reinstated in 1993).

After the release of *King Kong* in 1933, Gemora next became involved in a short, *King Kong* spoof that was unfortunately never finished: *The Lost Island*. (Also involved was one of *King Kong's* effects technicians, Orville Goldner.) The story was basically a humorous remake of *King Kong*, with explorers on the titular island coming across a giant ape that battles at least one dragon judging by photographs. As a musical comedy, it had several singing and dancing numbers. The film began production in 1934 by the Christie Studio. *The Lost Island* was to be a one-reel subject that would have been the first short film shot in Technicolor.

There were no actors to speak of, but would feature puppets made in the likeness of famous actors. For instance, the marionette for Ann Darrow was made to look like Mae West, and Carl Denham was based on Groucho Marx. These puppets were animated by the team of Charles Cristadoro, Mickey O'Rourke, James Blanding Sloan, and his adopted son Wah Ming Chang.

With Gemora obviously playing the Kong stand-in, the dragon was played by special effects sculptor Wah Chang. (Chang is of particular note because in the future he would go on to build props such as the tit-

One of Gemora's storyboards for THE LADY AND THE GORILLA.

ular object of George Pal's *The Time Machine* [1960], and other notable maquettes and props for films like *Planet of the Apes* [1968] as well as TV series like *Star Trek* and *Land of the Lost*.) Sadly, the spoof ended up costing the production company more than initially anticipated and so it was abandoned. Had the film been completed and released it may well have won an Oscar as the first short film shot in Technicolor. Instead that honor—and the Oscar—would go to *La Cucuracha*, a two-reel film directed by Pioneer Pictures for RKO, released later that year.

In the late 1930s, Gemora moved from Universal to Paramount, where he would work for the remainder of his career. It was around this time that Gemora proposed what would ultimately remain an unmade film: *The Lady and the Gorilla*.

Pitched in Paramount's Portrait Studio #1, it had everything you could want from a jungle picture including lions, hyenas, snakes, and an African jungle gorilla named Kimba. Gemora drew charcoal storyboards for each scene, one of which showed a deadly boa constrictor strangling one of the expedition's party to death. There was also to be a lion attack and "a blonde queen that sings and has a gorilla for a pet." [*Charlie Gemora Uncredited*] Gemora tried to drum up interest in the picture by taking photos with various starlets and also plenty of photos of the gorilla suit, including the animatronics that made the face move.

As the film's fate was debated by Paramount, Gemora did the *Perils of Pauline* (1947). That film cut out a scene of Gemora as a gorilla strangling Betty Hutton. "He has lost much of his ferocity in recent years. Censors no longer allow him to choke his victims — and for a good reason. Nearly all women in movie audiences identify themselves with the screen heroine. If she's being

More storyboards for THE LADY AND THE GORILLA depicting some exciting scenes.

kissed by Charles Boyer, well and good. But when Charlie Gemora gets his dukes on her throat, millions of women stagger out of theaters clutching their Adam's apples," the papers reported.

Gemora had hoped that *The Lady and the Gorilla* would be his next *Ingagi*, but due to the censor's reaction to *Perils of Pauline*, he gave up on the project.

By the late 1940s, playing apes in heavy, sweat inducing suits was getting a bit taxing for Gemora. Rather than playing apes in suits, he was becoming more interested in making movies of his own. This resulted in another unmade movie that sounded fantastic: *The Big Thaw*.

The Big Thaw was an ambitious idea that would have seen Ice Age monsters thawing out in the present day. Among them were some mammoths and a giant ape. Like the 1925 *Lost World*, the plan was probably to use stopmotion for the mammoths and the suit technique for the ape. (Would Gemora have played the creature? Who knows?)

The story was to be set in Siberia during a reversal of the North and South Poles. During the shift, creatures frozen during the Ice Age begin to thaw. As far as we can tell, the only creatures planned for the film were a herd of wooly mammoths and one giant ape. One of the mammoths would have a playful relationship with the protagonists. The ape was to be an antagonist who would try to abduct the girl a la' *King Kong*.

One of Gemora's storyboards for THE BIG THAW depicting a mammoth chasing some of the characters.

Overall, *The Big Thaw* was ahead of its time in terms of storyline, which is comparable to *The Day After Tomorrow* (2004). The main inspiration for the story was likely the frozen mammoth found in the Beresovca River in Siberia, which was so well preserved that it still had grass in its mouth in 1901. Gemora's treatment makes mention of people in Siberia eating the meat of frozen mammoths:

"It has been known to science that millions of years ago, the axis of the earth - the North and the South Poles were not in their position. The far north was once a tropical region. Time and time again large animals such as the mammoth elephant, the Mastodon has been discovered buried in the ice of the great Glacier of Siberia. It is known too that some of the people who live in that remote region of Siberia are actually mining fresh meat from the well preserved bodies of these tropical animals. They have found undigested vegetation in the stomachs of these animals - vegetation that can only be found in tropical countries. These animals had been frozen evidently in quick-freeze manner and are perfectly preserved."

As far as the production's timeline, many sources imply it was to be a feature film in the late 1940s. Gemo-

Storyboard showing the discovery of the frozen ape for THE BIG THAW, and later the ape on a rampage.

mammoths would be stop motion. Asked if any other ice age creatures beside Mammoths or giant apes would appear he replied, "That's all of the creatures I know of." And, as to the rumors of the lead actress, he also added, "And Anne Baxter is a guess as the character is named Ann Baxter."

Had the film been produced, it would have been unique for putting the spotlight on Ice Age mammals rather than prehistoric reptiles for once. Regardless of when *The Big Thaw* was dreamed up, in the 1950s, Gemora began planning an anthology TV series called *Mysteries of Life* similar to but predating *The Twilight Zone* (which premiered in 1959). Each week a different mystery would have been presented. Among the episode titles were "The Boiling

ra's relatives imply it was developed later, in 1957. Via Facebook, Jason Lee Barnett (producer of the documentary *Charlie Gemora Uncredited*) told me, "I believe [*Big Thaw*] is from circa 1957 and Anne Baxter was a possible lead (Gemora last working with her on *The Ten Commandments*)." Barnett also spoke to the effects, saying that since Gemora created the ape-man for *The Lost World* that the giant ape would probably be a man in a suit while the

THE LOST FILMS FANZINE #5 SPRING 2021

Watercolor by Gemora for "The Mystery of 100 Skeletons" for UNSOLVED MYSTERIES OF LIFE.

Flood of Guatemala", "The Death Battle of the Japanese Frogs", "The Shrimp of the Dry Desert", and also "Mining for Meat in Siberia." This is just my own hunch, but I would guess this episode was based upon frozen mammoths. (If that was the case, it may have been a condensed version of *The Big Thaw*. However, Gemora implied that he wanted this series to be based on real life mystery and lore, so while the mammoth aspect may have been explored, the giant ape likely would have been sidelined when it came to the TV iteration.)

As development continued, Gemora changed the title to *Unsolved Mysteries of Life*. His typed memo regarding the series read:

"Unsolved Mysteries of Life" is the title of a series intended for Television or for theatrical motion Pictures.

This series of shows is an idea in which mysterious events of the past, and present day travelogues, are worked together into one complete program. These events are based on actual facts.

The series can be inexpensively produced, studio made stock scenes, some of which could be in miniature, are added, to show flashbacks of the events.

As an example of this idea, the following is the script of the first episode, entitled "The Mystery of the 100 Skeletons"

15

Top: Charcoal storyboard by Gemora for "The Mystery of 100 Skeletons". Bottom: Gemora in PHANTOM OF THE RUE MORGUE (1954).

Other episodes to follow will be titled:

The Boiling Flood of Guatemala

The Death Battle of the Japanese Frogs

Mining for Meat in Siberia

The Shrimp of the Dry Desert

Mystery of the Inland Sea Gulls

"Material for future episodes is unlimited," he concluded. Sadly, the TV series never came to be.

Though he was no longer playing gorillas left and right, Gemora stayed active in the film world for the remainder of his career. Notably, in 1953, he not only sculpted some of the Martians for *War of the Worlds*, but he also played one. That same year he also worked on a 3-D remake of one of his early films: *Phantom of the Rue Morgue* (1954). As it turned out, it was his last appearance in a gorilla suit.

Five years later in 1961, at age 58, Gemora sadly passed away.

Though it's hard to believe today, Gemora never received much if any onscreen credit during his day, though film historians and gorilla movie lovers recognize his efforts now. Though it's not much, hopefully this meager article helps to acknowledge the indelible impact he made on the movie industry, especially in regards to giant apes and King Kong.

For more on the great Gemora, see J.L. Barnett's excellent 2016 documentary "Charlie Gemora: Uncredited" available to view on YouTube or charliegemora.com.

WANTED:
MORE INFORMATION ON THIS FILM!!!

Does this title sound familiar to you? Think maybe you've seen it, or know someone who has? To the best of our knowledge it was never produced, but if you know anything about it please write to the publisher at jplemay@plateautel.net or message us through Facebook at John LeMay's Lost Films: Book Series.

SNYDER'S SUPERHERO CORNER
SUPERMAN REBORN

BY TREVOR SNYDER

It shouldn't be so hard to make a good Superman movie.

Now, wait...allow me to clarify that. Of course, making any big-budget superhero movie is difficult on a number of logistical and financial reasons. I'm not oblivious to this, and am certainly not suggesting anyone should be able to just scrap together a camera, some friends, and a red cape and underwear, and then make a terrific film starring the world's most iconic superhero. What I am saying, however, is that the folks involved in bringing us the official versions of these movies – which, as we all know, is Warner Bros in this case – have been frustratingly overthinking (or in some cases, underthinking) effectively bringing Superman to a large mainstream audience for far too long now. This is evidenced not only by the misguided (in my opinion) attempt to Dark Knight-ize the character with 2013's *Man of Steel* and 2016's *Batman v Superman: Dawn of Justice*, but also reports that surfaced in 2020 regarding WB executives struggling to agree on a new direction to take the character in the wake of *Justice League's* box-office failure in 2017. According to these reports, the crux of the problem was that the studio just doesn't believe modern audiences want to watch blockbuster movies about such a straight-laced, morally upstanding hero...as if they somehow all failed to notice the MCU had just spent the past ten years making the world fall in love with Captain America, another character once often criticized and casually dismissed as a boring "boy scout."

This unfortunate failure to grasp what truly makes Superman special – and therefore feel an unnecessary desire to somehow "fix" him – has long plagued the character's cinematic journey, both in terms of the films that were made and, more notably for us, the ones that weren't. Superman is certainly not unique among his superhero peers in having a number of developed but even-

THE LOST FILMS FANZINE #5 SPRING 2021

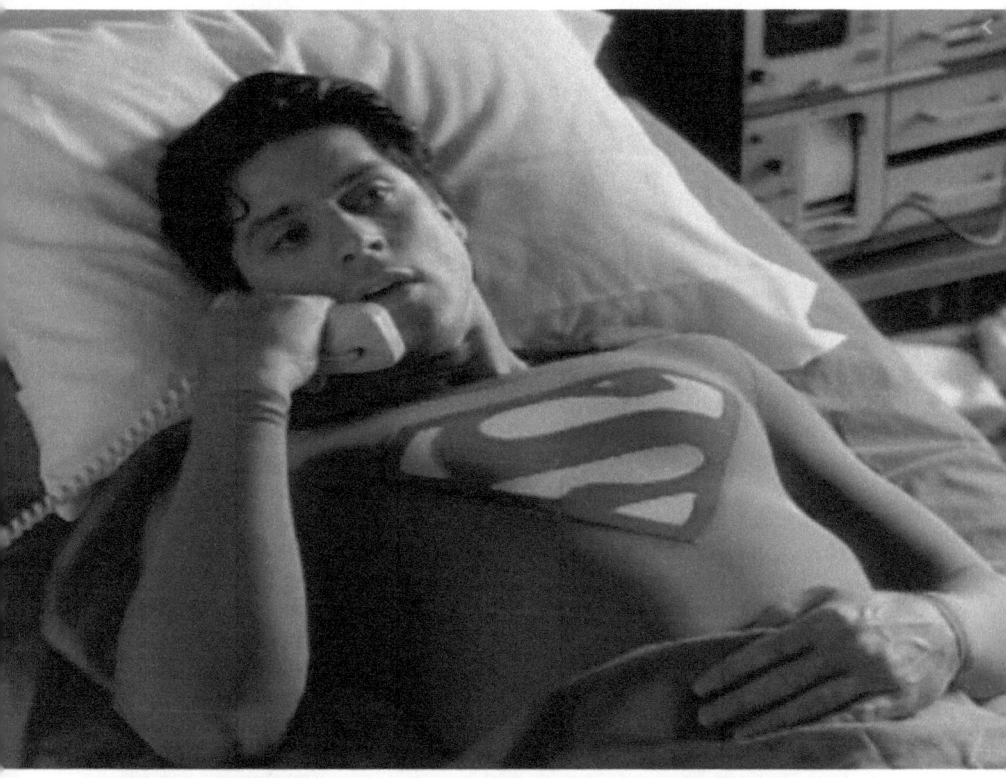

"Yeah, if we could actually get a good Superman script, that'd be grrreat," says Gerard Christopher to SUPERMAN REBORN and SUPERBOY writer Cary Bates over the phone. (Not really) Though it's possible that Christopher Reeve would have returned for the film, it's also possible that Gerard Christopher could have been cast. THE ADVENTURES OF SUPERBOY © 1989 DC Comics/Time Warner

tually aborted film projects over the decades, but what is striking when looking at many of the abandoned attempts at previous Superman movies is how often the writers took wild leaps and made jarring alterations to the character's look, personality, and world...especially in the nearly twenty-year development hell of a new Superman movie between 1987's *Superman IV* and 2006's *Superman Returns*. To be fair, the spectacular flame-out of the franchise with *Superman III* and *Superman IV* certainly didn't help the perception of Superman as an easily marketable marquee character during that time, and the second issue of this fanzine already chronicled the difficult and ultimately failed attempts of both Cannon Films and original Superman producers the Salkinds to get a fifth Christopher Reeve entry off the ground (pun not intended, but not regretted, either).

That article culminated with information on a *Superman V* script concerning Brainiac that producer Ilya Salkind and Cary Bates (a writer on the *Superboy* TV series of the 90s) had worked on. Despite plans to get this script before cameras in 1990, it never happened, and the Salkinds subsequently lost their rights to the character in 1992. And yet, the Salkind/Bates Brainiac story remained

very much in the mix at Warner Bros. as a potential relaunch for the franchise...at least for a time. Today I'm looking at a 1992 draft of the script – titled *Superman Reborn* – credited to Cary Bates and Mark Jones (a fellow *Superboy* writer but, way more importantly, also the writer/director of *Leprechaun!*). Though the previous article gave a brief idea of the film's plot, the full script is interesting enough (both good and bad) to be worthy of a closer examination.

The script starts with an admittedly badass opening sequence in which we are introduced to Brainiac, a powerful AI/giant robot-machine piloting a giant spaceship through the galaxy (in a very nice touch, the script describes him thusly: "if Satan himself ever decided to forge a machine out of the molten depths of Hell...it would look something like BRAINIAC"). We come upon Brainiac as he is multitasking – learning about Earth by watching transmissions of classic TV shows like *I Love Lucy* and *The Lone Ranger*, and contemplating whether to save the young children inhabitants of a gravely damaged spaceship that has sent out the distress signal he has just responded to. It seems the children's ship was attacked by intergalactic slavers that kidnapped their parents and left them for dead. Brainiac's perpetually put-upon alien subordinate, Kosmo (I know... not exactly a name that screams "alien sidekick," but we'll just have to accept it), pleads for his master to spare and save the children, but after a scan of their ship reveals that he already knows everything he needs to about their culture, Brainiac instead blasts their craft to pieces, murdering them. "My function is to learn," Brainiac explains, "their species had nothing to teach me." It's a terrific, shocking opener, quickly and effectively setting up both our villain's motivations and how much of a threat he can be.

Kosmo, we will later learn, accidentally played a hand in Brainiac's creation, but has since – for centuries now – been held captive as an unwilling assistant, helping his master travel the universe to not only learn about various alien civilizations, but also to "collect" samples... which Brainiac does by shrinking entire cities and their inhabitants and teleporting them into egg-like globes within his ship. Following the destruction of the young aliens in their stranded ship, Kosmo decides that he has finally had enough of his captor and enacts a calculated plan, drawing Brainiac's attention to Earth, and more specifically Metropolis. Kosmo knows Brainiac will be intrigued by Superman and want to study him, and also secretly hopes that Superman's powers and innate goodness will once and for all be Brainiac's downfall.

An evil super-robot coming to Earth to conquer humanity would be bad news for our hero even on his best day, but – wouldn't you know it – this story just also happens to be taking place while Superman is dealing with distracting relationship issues. Despite a moment in which the *Daily Planet* newsroom is described as now being "hi-tech" for containing such incredible items as modems and faxes(!), the movie is otherwise set at an indeterminate time in the character's timeline (most likely so that it could work both as a *Superman V* and a reboot). But it's made clear that Superman and Lois Lane have been "a thing" for quite some time, and lately Lois has been growing tired of his inability to settle down and commit. Superman is definitely upset about this, so much so that he almost caves and reveals his big secret (that he is actually Clark Kent, which Lois is still unaware of) to her, but he chickens out at the last moment and can only look on as a dejected Lois accepts a new job in LA, planning to start a new chapter in her life away from Metropolis and her now super-ex.

Eventually, Brainiac makes it to Earth and wastes no time enclosing Metropolis in an impenetrable bubble, shrinking it down, and bringing it onboard his ship to join his menagerie of intergalactic cities. Braniac is not satisfied with simply observing humanity through glass, however, preferring "close observation at the most intimate level." He has Kosmo make him a cloned human body for his electronic mind to inhabit, shrink down, and visit the city. This leads to a nifty bit where Braniac, now in an actual living, breathing body for the first time in his existence, begins to experience human emotions, which he finds fascinating (though he ultimately decides to simply "delete" the pesky emotions he feels he has no need for, such as "remorse"). He finds the new emotion of "anger" to be particularly exciting, and it fuels his first confrontation with Superman, in which he handily defeats our hero on the streets of Metropo-

Far Left: Issue of ACTION COMICS with Braniac gracing the cover. Above: Trading card featuring Braniac. Background: Braniac's ship as envisioned for Tim Burton's aborted SUPERMAN LIVES. *Superman co-creator Jerry Siegal Superman © DC Comics and the heirs of*

lis, as its confused (finding yourself suddenly cut off from the world in a giant bubble will do that to you) and worried citizens – including Lois, Perry White, and Jimmy Olsen – look on. Brainiac appears to obliterate Superman before everyone's eyes, and in a funny, super-dickish move, erects a steel statue of a cowering, defeated Superman at that spot, with a plaque that reads "In Memory of the Specimen Superman. Origin Unknown."

But wait! Killing off Superman at the 45-minute mark might at first seem like a shockingly brave story move, but I hope you're not too surprised to learn that Superman is, in fact, alive. It turns out that, at the last second before his mole-

LOIS AND CLARK, which debuted not long after this script was shelved, also utilized a "Lois copy" storyline where Lex Luthor cloned Lois, took the real thing for himself, and stuck Clark with the clone in "Double Jeopardy." (Season 3, Episode 16) Lois and Clark: The New Adventures of Superman © Warner Media/DC Comics

cules could be destroyed, he was in fact intercepted and beamed into another of Brainiac's shrunken cities...which is soon revealed as none other than Kandor, the last surviving city of Superman's birth-planet, Krypton! How did they manage this trick, you might ask? Well, in a real "screenwriting coincidence" touch, one of the city's leaders reveals to Superman that every city in Brainiac's collection is afforded a closely monitored but nonetheless rationed amount of teleportation beams. I mean, look, I'm not one to tell supervillains how to conduct their business, but this certainly seems like a bad call on Brainiac's

part. And sure enough, it has bit him on the butt here, as Superman is now able to recover from his battle among his own kind. To his dismay, however, Superman discovers that these Kryptonians, who are aware of Krypton's destruction not long after their capture, now (somewhat understandably) view Brainiac as a savior figure to their culture. The leaders of Kandor, including Max-Dur, an old friend of Superman's father, Jor-El, are eager to convince Superman to forget about his past life on Earth and instead accept a new life here among his own people, where he can finally simply be Kal-El. This doesn't sit well with our boy

THE LOST FILMS FANZINE #5 SPRING 2021

This panel from SUPERMAN'S GIRLFRIEND, LOIS LANE #134 shows the titular character inspecting the bottled city of Kandor, which Lois was slated to visit in SUPERMAN REBORN. © Warner Media/DC Comics

in blue, however – not only does he no longer have his powers under the simulated red sun of Krypton (leading to some compelling moments where he bleeds and experiences pain and exhaustion for the first time *[which would seem to ignore the events of* Superman II-*Ed.]*), but he still has unfinished business with Brainiac, and so he escapes the Kandor science council and goes on the run in the city, looking for a way to escape the bubble and find his way back to his loved ones.

And not a moment too soon, really, as in the meantime, Brainiac's still emerging emotions have caused him to take an interest in Lois, who he is fascinated by primarily because "you were Superman's woman." Brainiac decides he will explore the human concepts of love by removing Lois from the enclosed Metropolis, restore her to normal size, and woo her aboard his ship. This is when it begins to become dismayingly clear that a good amount of this script's run-time is going to be devoted to awkward, cringe-worthy, and sometimes outright creepy sequences of Brainiac trying to seduce Lois, such as a bizarre sequence where she is forced to attend a formal-dress dinner with him on the ship's observation deck. There's some occasionally

amusing attempted comedy here, such as one of Brainiac's robot helpers, Vincent, wearing an apron and chef's hat and trying to replicate Earth food, only to inadvertently disgust Lois by serving her a blue steak. But as Brainiac becomes more and more obsessed with possessing Lois and getting her to consent to a physical relationship, these sequences really just drag the film down, and you realize what initially seemed like what could be an incredible morality play between Superman and Brainiac has instead devolved into little more than an annoying "unrequited love triangle" story.

Because screenwriters love ticking clocks, another plot element is revealed wherein Brainiac tells Lois that he is slowly sapping Metropolis of its air supply, believing that she will be better able to love him if she loses all her previous connections to Earth. Why he wouldn't immediately just blow up the shrunken city instead of drawing the process out is, of course, a great question...but then we wouldn't be able to periodically cut back to Jimmy Olsen and Perry White finally bonding as they draw nearer to death. Eventually Lois teams with Kosmo to secretly and temporarily distract Brainiac with a life-like Lois android, while Kosmo

23

Above: Superman comes to blows with Brainiac in one of the comics. Background page opposite: Suit design for SUPERMAN REBORN, though possibly for a later iteration rather than version discussed here.
© Warner Media/DC Comics

manages to shrink Lois down and send her into Kandor to find Superman. Brainiac learns of the deception (which at least leads to a cool reveal when Brainiac starts making out with the Lois-bot, realizes something is amiss, and decapitates it onscreen before the audience is aware it's not actually our heroine), tortures Kosmo to death, and then once again miniaturizes himself and proceeds to give chase into Kandor.

While Superman, Lois, and Max-Dur flee Brainiac inside Kandor, making their way to a secret exit that Max-Dur knows about (again, Brainiac really needs to work on his set-up here), Vincent and his fellow robot companion Roberto (I know, I know...like I said, names are not this script's greatest strength) secretly redirect Brainiac's ship back to the devastated world of Colu, where Brainiac was first created, and where he initially gained sentience and laid waste to the planet and population alike. It is on the surface of Colu that Superman and Brainiac, having now both made their way out of the Kandor bubble, engage in their final, knock-down, drag-out battle. The script has already drawn attention to Superman's explicit creed never to take a life (sorry, *Man of Steel* fans), and this pays off when he refuses to kill a defeated Brainiac even as the villain begs him to. When Superman says no, Brainiac simply picks up a shard of metal and stabs himself in the neck, to Superman's dismay. But this turns out to be a ruse, as Brainiac has simply killed his human body so that his consciousness can return to his larger, more powerful robot body, allowing for one more big action sequence with Superman taking on a giant machine-brain. Oddly enough, the movie immediately forgets about the "Superman never kills" rule that it just referenced only a few pages ago, as Superman ultimately defeats Brainiac by using the robot's technology to once again shrink himself, fly inside Brainiac's head, and then enlarge a metal shard he has brought with him so that it not only pierces through the villain's electronic brain, but also causes an explosion "so awesome the planet Colu is obliterated." Huh. I guess maybe Superman saw that initial human-body-Brainiac suicide as a clever way to overlook his sacred rule on a technicality?

Anyway, in the final pages, we learn that Vincent and Roberto have built a new robot body for Kosmo's consciousness, and Brainiac's grateful and now freed former slave returns Metropolis to its rightful size and place on Earth. Kosmo agrees to return the other cities to their own planets, and find a "New Krypton" for Kandor – there's a nice beat where Superman looks in on the fellow Kryptonians to say goodbye, ensuring them they will always be in his heart even though he still considers Earth his real home now. Back on Earth, Lois and Superman make up, and as a sign that he is finally ready to give her the sort of relationship she wants, he not only reveals his secret identity to her, but also asks her to marry him, which she gladly accepts. The film ends with Superman and Lois flying toward the camera, giving the audience a wink before departing into the night.

On a purely conceptual level, there is some stuff to enjoy about this script. For one thing, it's nice to see Brainiac given center stage as the primary antagonist, even if this isn't necessarily the most compelling version of him. I think a lot of Superman fans would join me in arguing for Brainiac as Superman's second most memorable/formidable villain (at least top five, if you're not willing to go that far); it's pretty darn surprising he has not yet appeared in any of Superman's eight big screen appearances. He has fared better on the small screen, as versions of him have shown up in both *Smallville*, *Supergirl*, and *Krypton*, and in various animated Superman projects, including the DC Universe Animated film *Superman: Unbound*...which is not only basically a better version of the *Superman Reborn* story, but is – in this author's opinion – right up there with the first two Christopher Reeve movies as one of the best Superman films we have gotten yet. To his credit, Ilya Salkind wanted to use Brainiac as early as *Superman III*, and his "Story by" credit here is almost certainly partly due to his dogged attempts to finally get the murderous robot on the big screen. Having Brainiac spend most of the movie in a cloned human body, wooing Lois and wrestling with his emerging emotions, seems like more of an excuse to let a name actor ham it up than it is a chance to really explore what makes Brainiac such a compelling character in the comics, but it is sort of fun to imagine which actor of the time might have ended up with the role (I might be crazy here, but I kept picturing him as early 90s era Bruce Willis, bringing some of that madcap *Death Becomes Her* energy).

And speaking of Superman villains,

THE LOST FILMS FANZINE #5 SPRING 2021

Like many a Superman film before it, SUPERMAN REBORN was set to end with a shot of Superman and Lois flying above the earth. SUPERMAN IV: THE QUEST FOR PEACE © 1987 Warner Media/DC Comics

I have to admit I also enjoyed reading a Superman script that didn't feature Lex Luthor (or an obvious Lex Luthor surrogate, like Robert Vaughn's Ross Webster from *Superman III*). Sure, I love Lex, and yes, he is THE most important Superman villain and a crucial element of his world, but it's always been far too easy for Superman stories to fall back on him as the only significant villain. If he had showed up here, even in a secondary role, it would have only taken attention away from Brainiac, so it was a good call to just give old Brainy the entire spotlight to himself.

I'll also give credit where credit is due and say there are a fair number of enjoyable, memorable scenes throughout the script. I particularly liked an early Metropolis sequence where Lois and Clark are caught in the middle of an attempted bank robbery. Not able to make a costume change without giving away his secret, Clark instead slyly uses a number of his superpowers on the downlow in order to foil the crook, including a great moment where he uses his super speed to catch a bullet headed toward Lois in his teeth. This culminates with a funny beat where the bank guard says to Clark, "You okay, pal? For a minute there, I was sure he was gonna make you eat a bullet," as Clark swallows the .357 slug to hide the evidence of his super act.

That all said, though, it's impossible to read the entire script and not ultimately come away considering it a series of missed opportunities. As I said before, primarily portraying Brainiac as a lovesick creep angry that Lois won't sleep with him is just about the worst possible representation of the character possible, especially given how deep one could have gone with the character. There's some brief lip-service given to the idea that human emotions have made Brainiac even more evil than he initially was, which is a fascinating idea, but the script doesn't bother to explore it in any sustained

26

fashion. And while Brainiac's vast intellect has always been what makes him such a formidable foe for Superman, every confrontation with him here essentially boils down to a slugfest where Superman just has to beat him up hard enough to win. There's no real convincing sense of Superman perhaps being out of his league, which is what you want from a supposedly frightening villain like Brainiac.

Equally aggravating is the treatment of Superman's adventures in Kandor. Superman has spent his entire life believing he was the last living Kryptonian...you would think the discovery of an entire city of fellow Kryptonians would be an incredible, mind-altering experience for him. But the story immediately puts him at angry odds with the city's Science Council, and his entire time there is spent trying to escape from them, or on the run and visibly upset that the citizens now celebrate "Brainiac Day" in celebration of their supposed savior. There are no sequences depicting Kal-El really exploring this piece of his homeworld; no moments where he engages with the city or its people to learn more about his birth-culture. Heck, we don't even get a moment where he is allowed to learn more about his late father from Max-Dur, even though the two spend some time together and the script makes clear that Max-Dur and Jor-El were colleagues.

Perhaps even more bothersome, though, is the script's overall treatment of its female characters. To say this is a problematic script on a gender level would be putting it mildly. There are only three female characters, only one of whom survives, and all three are framed almost entirely in their relation to more important male characters. First, we have Kosmo's wife, Krynna, who I didn't even mention during my recap because she is so inconsequential – she's a fellow prisoner who only has a couple early brief dialogue exchanges with her husband before being murdered by Brainiac (by turning her into a melting pile of goo while Kosmo is embracing her) after he discovers his subordinate's betrayal. Then there's Kandor citizen Lyla, who Kal-El first encounters being assaulted by an alien thug known as a Slubber while on the run and hiding in the city. Kal-El saves her from the attack; she takes him back to her place and immediately puts the moves on him (we learn that her husband died not long before, but that doesn't mean she's powerless against Superman's raw machismo). He of course rebuffs her, and much of Lyla's remaining screen-time is spent depicting her as incredibly jealous of Lois, who she has never even met. I was really confused about why this character is even in the script at all – she supplies Superman with some convenient invisibility pills (no, really) that you just know will come into play during a later confrontation with Brainiac (spoiler: they do), and tells him about her uncle, who she says is an important scientist who might be able to help Kal-El escape Kandor. But as soon as they make their way to her uncle's location, he is killed by Brainiac before even getting a line of dialogue, leaving one to wonder why Lyla herself couldn't have just been the scientist with the knowledge of Kandor technology, instead of only a horny, jealous victim. In a final indignity, Lyla tries to betray Superman once she sees him reunited with Lois, pledging her loyalty to Brainiac only to have him murder her in return (though I admit I do love his line here: "Never interrupt your god when he's having a tantrum").

Until Superman and Braniac meet on the big screen, the animated SUPERMAN UNBOUND provides an excellent encounter between the two. © 2013 Warner Media/DC Comics

Although Lois at least survives the film, giving her something of an advantage over Krynna and Lyla, it's still undeniably disheartening to see one of comics' toughest, most entertaining heroines relegated here to little more than an object of affection being fought over by the hero and villain. On top of that, Lois's annoyance with Superman's duty to his work paints her in a really negative light here. There certainly is a sympathetic and believable way to talk about the frustrating nature of dating someone who is often needed elsewhere, one that could have made Lois feel more real and relatable. Instead, the script takes the lazy and oft-repeated (especially in superhero literature) shortcut of simply showing her as being dismissively aggrieved that Superman is usually busier saving the world than spending quality time with her. In fact, the script's final straw for Lois – the moment that leads her to decide to leave Superman and move away from the city – is that he flies away from a conversation they are having in order to go save a group of children from a burning building. I mean, c'mon Lois...I think we can probably let that one slide, right?

All in all, *Superman Reborn* is an occasionally fun, but primarily frustrating read. I can't say I'm too disappointed it was never made, though I'll concede it still would have been a better cinematic send-off for Christopher Reeve (if he had agreed to return) than *Superman IV: Quest for Peace*...though that's a pretty low bar to clear. It's a fairly boring version of a classic good vs. evil match-up from the comics, but at least it often seems to have its heart in the right place and doesn't overly disrespect the character of Superman or do anything too outrageous to his mythology. That's more than can be said for some of the other unfilmed Superman scripts that would eventually follow. In fact, to that point, this isn't the end of the *Superman Reborn* saga, as two years later Warner Bros hired writer Jonathan Lemkin to deliver a new version of the script, and then Lemkin's version was subsequently retooled and rewritten by Gregory Poirier. These two new scripts would retain the *Superman Reborn* title and some of the plot elements established by Salkind, Bates, and Jones... but would each also offer wild and sometimes unbelievable new story developments. I'll be back to look at those *Superman Reborn* scripts in a later issue. For now, let's all just keep our eyes to the sky and keep patiently waiting for the great Superman movie we deserve.

251 million years ago she nearly wiped out life on Earth. Now she is back to try again. Vistakill! Even kaiju flee from her. Can she be stopped?

Grab your copy on Amazon.com

AVAILABLE NOW

In this 360 page, large format, full colour new book from *We Belong Dead* we look at the wonderful world of monstrous giant creatures: King Kong and his kith and kin, Godzilla and the Kaijus, Dragons, Dinosaurs & Lost Worlds, Giant Bugs, and Nature Bites Back. Packed with rare stills, posters and lobby cards, this is bound to be another hit!

LIMITED EDITION - ORDER NOW

WWW.WEBELONGDEAD.CO.UK

A We Belong Dead Presentation

MIKADO ZOMBIE
HOW REAL-LIFE TRAGEDY CHANGED THE COURSE OF A FILM
BY MATTHEW B. LAMONT

This is the story of how a circumstance can influence a filmmaker to change course on his creation. In 1989, Tomoo Haraguchi, a make-up artist, came up with an idea for a horror movie called *Mikado Zombie*. It's about a Japanese World War II soldier that rises from the dead as a zombie and starts bringing fear and terror to the people of modern Japan. Props were being made for this movie, including the title character. Everything was ready for the independently produced project, but something caused it to come to a screeching halt. At the moment when filming was about to start, there were reports about a serial killer named Tsutomu Miyazaki. (No relation to Hayao Miyazaki, a famous Japanese animator.)

It was said that in the late-eighties, Tsutomu murdered four girls between the ages of four to seven. Four-year-old Mari Konno on August 22nd, 1988, seven-year-old Masami Yoshizawa on October 3rd, 1988, four-year-old Erika Namba on December 12th, 1988, and five-year-old Ayako Nomoto on June 6th, 1989. These killings were known as "The Little Girl Murders". This lead to Mr. Miyazaki's arrest on July 23rd, 1989 where the media gave him such names as "The Killer Nerd" and "The Otaku Murderer."

The trial started on March 30, 1990, and ended with his execution on June 17, 2008. There was a lot of proof that led to the origins of his murders. It was detailed on the news that when his home was being searched, they found out that there were a lot of videos ranging from anime, horror, and slasher movies.

Due to this, the horror genre was a tendentious subject in Japan at that time causing it to be the nail in the coffin for *Mikado Zombie*. It was a case of reality damaging a movie's production. This caused Tomoo Haraguchi, with the help of Junki Takegami, to change it to a science fiction movie about a World War II-era cyborg resurrected in the present, thus *Mikadroid* (1991) was

31

Director Tomoo Haraguchi.

born. The film came out on DVD in America as *Mikadroid: Robokill at Discoclub Layla*. The film was about an underground science lab in World War II Japan where three highly athletic chosen men were experimented on to create a cyborg soldier. While two escaped during the war, only to be killed by the bomb, the last android warrior survived, but was never activated.

Years passed and all was forgotten. The place where the lab was located, became a discotheque called Discoclub Layla. Due to the faulty basement generator, the android is activated and goes on a killing spree in the basement! As for some trivia, this film featured an appearance by famous little person, Little Man Machan, who was known for playing Minya in the Showa Godzilla franchise. The special effects were made by Shinji Higuchi, who directed the special effects for Shuske Kaneko's Gamera trilogy in the 90's and co-directed *Shin-Godzilla* (2016).

From my point of view, the moral to this story is: If something doesn't work for one reason, try a smarter alternative. However, here is the main moral to the story: Remember how the serial killer was influenced by the horror genre, which led him to commit crimes? You should not feed your mind with horror, terror, and murders. One must be careful with that sort of entertainment. Slasher movies are not for everyone despite their popularity.

It was a wise choice from Haraguchi and Takegami to change from a bland run-of-the-mill horror movie to an imaginative science-fiction film. Roger Dickens, who's special effects credits includes, *Land That Time Forgot* (1975) and *Warlords of Atlantis* (1978), said that slasher movies are unimaginative and horrible. Dale Kuipers, a make-up artist on *The Howling* (1981), and stop-motion model maker for the live-action cartoon, *Caveman* (1981), said in a 1984 TV interview, that he considered slasher movies to be stupid because they inspired people to become monsters. He went on to say that films like *King Kong* (1933), *Jason and Argonauts* (1963), and kaiju films (such as Godzilla), inspire people to create monsters (and perhaps end up going into the field of special effects). Tim Paxton, the creator of the magazine, *Monster*, despises them, as does the writer of this article.

Some ideas are better left untouched and some films, such as those of the slasher genre, are better left unwatched in my opinion!

The Theatre of What Should Have Been
by Stan Hyde

PART 3 OF 3
WAR OF THE WORLDS

In 1978, 80 years after the appearance of the novel and 40 years after the Orson Welles broadcast, at the height of the popularity of the 'Concept Album' in which songs are linked by narrative or theme, Jeff Wayne produced a two record set based on *The War of the Worlds*.

Overall, the album is a great addition to the history of adaptations of Wells' novel, featuring actors alongside rock musicians to dramatize the story of Martian carnage. Sir Richard Burton was 'the narrator,' assisted by stage star Julie Covington, alongside musicians like Justin Hayward of The Moody Blues and David Essex.

John L. Flynn in his book *War of the World: from Wells to Spielberg* describes the album as "not so much a concept album as a rite of passage" citing "the death screams in the grooves, the ravens pecking at red Martian flesh in the sleeve booklet, or simply the distorted shrieks of 'Ulla.'"

According to Jeff Wayne, interviewed in Flynn's excellent book, Paramount approached him about a film version in 1979. (Apparently later, when preparing his 2005 version, Spielberg also thought adapting the musical would be a fine idea, although he was only interested in a straight version.)

Wayne says, "We tried to develop a film project with Paramount but they're a big corporation and musicals are not necessarily always the big successes that they could be. We've just never been able to together with them, although we've had great success in a lot of other media and the album keeps selling and the singles keep getting reinterpreted. My vision has remained for over 20 years of how it would be done as a film and now there are all these things that have grown up in that world of technology which would make it that much more exciting. The vision is still as clear to me today as it was all that time ago."

Between 2006 and 2008, another attempt was made to develop the project. Wayne feels it was still viable since his version is a period

Fabulous album cover for JEFF WAYNE'S MUSICAL VERSION OF THE WAR OF THE WORLDS above, and in the background and on the previous page are photos from a live stage performance.

retelling of the story and not a modern version like Spielberg's. Script, storyboards and sample CGI footage were created to help present the project, which also include a prequel that explained why the Martians were forced abandon Mars and seek out a new life on Earth.

The film would have been budgeted at around 48 million dollars, and be entirely accomplished with CGI animation. Some test of concept videos can be seen on YouTube, and there are storyboard samples on Twitter and elsewhere.

Wayne owns worldwide rights to his musical version and some ancillary rights to the original novel, and so development of video games has occurred in the past, and the idea of a theme park has even been floated. In 2012, Jeff Wayne's Musical Version of *The War of the Worlds - The New Generation* was released as an album and a live tour, with some new content. Liam Neeson now appears holographically as the Narrator, replacing the late Sir Richard Burton. A DVD of the concert - which ran until 2014 - is available, and later a theatrical version played at the Dominion Theatre in London's West End in 2016.

The True Story of the Martian Invasion tour dates are set for 2021, but the invaders may have met their

Two CGI stills from the aborted film version of the musical, and a storyboard.

match because of the worldwide Covid-19 pandemic (and how is that for ironic?!)

In 1986, George A. Romero adapted H.G. Wells' novel in a screenplay titled *War of the Worlds, The Night They Came* for a production to be produced with Dario Argento. No stranger to monster invasions, the *Night Of The Living Dead* director based his work closely on the novel with a focus on the human interaction during the invasion, a feature of most of his horror films.

Apparently the story focused on a young girl named Rachel staying with her grandfather when the Martian invasion begins. Rachel is a smart ten year old, but needs the comfort of her grandfather in the terrifying situation. In an attempt to escape the carnage, they meet and join a small group of refugees.

These are Dr. Byron Forrester, a 60 year old astronomer who is a World War II veteran, and a bit like an older Indiana Jones character. (Is he a relation to Dr. Clayton Forester?) Dr. Forrester's young apprentice is Dr. Sylvia Robinson (hmm, Sylvia Van Buren and Ann Robinson), a smart, strong young woman who shares a firm, sisterly bond with Rachel ultimately. The final member of the group is Dr. Robert Pryor, who grew up with Forrester, served in World War II with him, and studied at the same collage. He is a smart nerd - the intellectual hero. Ultimately they end up all hiding in the basement of a character named Dior Draven.

Draven was to be a 45 year old big game hunter, a 'man's man,' and a great shot with a rifle. In the script, he is at odds with Mitch 'Chevelle' Sampson, a 61 year old World War II veteran. (His nickname comes from his love for his '67 Chevelle SS.) Another 'man's man,' Chevelle and Draven just naturally rub each other the wrong way.

It appears the film would have featured the classic 'alien tripod' had it been produced. Besides focusing on the adventures of this band of refugees, action would be intercut with the battles of five-star general Herbert Mann, who is age 72. A combination of General George S. Patton and General Douglas MacArthur he will do anything to stop the Martian war machines, regardless of the cost.

As is common in Romero's scripts where human monsters are often contrasted with real monsters, General Mann is the film's antagonist. An interesting element of the script - besides the obvious tips of the hat to George Pal's movie and the very *Night of the Living Dead* hiding in the basement motif - is the general age of the characters.

Since the film was proposed for 1986, the focus on older characters with a history of serving in World War II suggests that Romero's often satirical eye was focused on the 'greatest generation.'

Over the years, it seems, the versions of *The War of the Worlds* that have been successful have been the versions that connect most viscerally to the social unease and fears of the audience of the time. Hence the success of the Pal film and the Spielberg film. Though at times 'period' adaptations of Wells have been fairly successful, like Pal's *The Time Machine* or Ray Harryhausen's *The First Men In The Moon*, the real driving force of the narrative in terms of *The War of the Worlds* is the unease generated by seeing man put in his place by a superior intelligence that is, finally, as ruthless as mankind is.

To be truly effective, I think, the story needs a contemporary background, and the history of the successful film adaptations of Wells' novel seems to bear this out.

The unmade films tended to have a fair amount of distraction added to the plot, whether it was the focus on the love triangle that marred the earliest attempts by DeMille and Paramount, or the space opera complications of the George Pal television series.

At the end of the day it is the fear of war that gives the story it's emotional subtext, and the recognition from the audience that the fearful colonizing monsters are really a funhouse mirror representation of ourselves and our own inhumanity. Whether it was the colonization of Tasmania, the fear of the cold war and nuclear destruction, or the unease surrounding 911 and the Iraq war, the story works best when we see ourselves in the metaphor of the martians and the fear of the warlike, colonialist monsters that we can be, as represented by the dark parable of 'survival of the fittest.'

The story begins and ends as a reflection of our fears, and though it ends happily, in the end it is nature itself and the vagaries of evolution, and not our efforts, that saves us.

"For so it had come about, as indeed I and many men might have foreseen had not terror and disaster blinded our minds. These germs of disease have taken toll of humanity since the beginning of things--taken toll of our prehuman ancestors since life began here. But by virtue of this natural selection of our kind we have developed resisting power; to no germs do we succumb without a struggle, and to many--those that cause putrefaction in dead matter, for instance--our living frames are altogether immune. But there are no bacteria in Mars, and directly these invaders arrived, directly they drank and fed, our microscopic allies began to work their overthrow. Already when I watched them they were irrevocably doomed, dying and rotting even as they went to and fro. It was inevitable. By the toll of a billion deaths man has bought his birthright of the earth, and it is his against all comers; it would still be his were the Martians ten times as mighty as they are. For neither do men live nor die in vain."

***

For those crazy completists who actually want to see the versions of The War Of The Worlds *that actually were made...*

Besides the big screen adaptations in 1953 and 2005, several other adaptations of *The War of the Worlds* exist for those folks who want to complete their viewing of various versions.

Of course, the 1988 - 1990 television series is a semi-sequel to the original George Pal film and does seem to have some elements that might have been inspired by his pitch for a series (although honestly the second season plot twist that there is more than one alien race involved is so convenient for a continuing series that it probably arose independently). In the series the aliens from the 1953 invasion, thought to be dead, are simply dormant and appear again.

The 2019 adaptation of *The War of the Worlds* by Mammoth Screen for the BBC is set in Edwardian England and is an attempt to follow events in the novel with some changes of character from the novel. (The main focus character is a journalist and a conscious attempt was made to "give the male character a wife who had strength of character in her own right," says writer Peter Harness. Essentially this is a mini-series version of the book

Another 2019 adaptation of *The War of the Worlds* is a (possibly) continuing series from Fox Networks Group and StudioCanal. (It is an 8 part series set in contemporary times.) Like the Spielberg adaptation, it foregoes Mars as the source of the invasion. It first premiered in France in October 2019, and has been renewed for a second season, although production has been delayed due to the pandemic.

As described by Den of Geek "In this new take on *War Of The Worlds*, when astronomers detect a transmission from another star, it is definitive proof of intelligent extra-terrestrial life. Earth's population waits for further contact with bated breath, but does not have to wait long. Within days, mankind is all but wiped out, with just pockets of humanity are left in an eerily deserted world. As alien ships appear in the sky, the survivors ask a burning question — who are these attackers and why are they hell-bent on our destruction?"

There have also been a number of Direct-to-Video adaptations which I will list here for those who might want to seek them out.

(1981) ***The War of the Worlds: Next Century*** Piotr Szulkin's Polish adaptation. Among Direct-To-Video films, this is interesting because it was banned by the Polish government because it was clearly a political satire that showed the State collaborating with the martians to the point of encouraging people to donate blood to feed them.

The film has been presented as

part of a retrospective at the Lincoln Center and is one of the four films in Piotr Szulkin (4 DVD) The Masterpieces of Polish Cinema - a Pal DVD

(2005) *H.G. Wells' The War Of The Worlds* Produced by Pendragon Pictures. This film very much rode the wave of publicity generated for the Spielberg film. It is set in Victorian England in 1898. There were generally poor reviews and even some controversy as the production company produced a press release claiming that there were visual similarities between the production and the Dark Horse Comics publication H. G. Wells' *The War of the Worlds*. Pendragon Productions set up an internet poll to query fans about similarities, but later apologized for 'any misconception its press release or later internet poll may have caused.' At lease one reviewer summoned the name of 'Ed Wood' when reviewing the film, but opinions vary. (Released on DVD)

(2005) *H.G. Wells' War of the Worlds* Also riding the wave of the Spielberg publicity machine was Asylum pictures version directed by David Michael Latt. Set in the United States in the current day, the film was released on DVD one day before Spielberg's picture premiered, the common strategy of the company. (My favourite was their release of *Atlantic Rim* to cash in on Del Toro's *Pacific Rim*. Not since the days of Roger Corman's New World films, and wave riding production like *Carnosaur* riding the wake of *Jurassic Park* has there been a company quite so comfortable about producing blatant rip-offs.)

(2008) *War of the Worlds 2: The Next Wave* Asylum produced a sequel to follow up their original 'mockbuster.' This time the Martians create a wormhole between Earth and Mars for another series of attacks.

Both these films were released on DVD.

(2012) *War of the Worlds: The True Story* Another Pendrgon Pictures version of the story, this time in documentary style presenting the reminiscences of the survivors of the Martian war. Director Timothy Hines cites the Orson Welles radio broadcast as an inspiration for the 'true story' approach. Unlike Pendragon Pictures 2005 version, this version saw fairly decent reviews in its limited release. (Released on DVD in 2013)

(2012) *War of the Worlds: Goliath* This Malaysian animated film, directed by Joe Pearson is centred around a human operated tripod - 'Goliath' - used to battle the invaders. As described by Wikipedia, "It has become a dieselpunk/steampunk-like world, where Earth is at the potential onset of the Great War as the European nations' fragile alliance begins to shatter. Eric Wells is Captain of a Tripod squad for the A.R.E.S. (Allied Resistance Earth Squadron) organization, alongside American Lieutenant Jennifer Carter, Irish Corporal Patrick O'Brien, Canadian Sergeant Abraham Douglas, and Malayan Lieutenant Raja Iskandar Shah. A.R.E.S. is commanded by strict Russian General Sergei Kushnirov (who lost his family to the Martians in 1899 at St. Petersburg), Secretary of War Theodore Roosevelt (who forsook a second term as President of the United States), and Professor Nikola Tesla, an enigmatic scientist who reverse-engineered the technology from the first, failed, invasion of the Martians and created

A.R.E.S. weapons and vehicles.

Eric Wells is given the first of a new type of steam-powered, Achilles-class Battle Tripod, (65 feet tall, armed with heavy machine guns and six light rockets, a heat ray and an 88-millimeter cannon) who nicknames his new tripod 'The Goliath'.

Sounds cool (I have not seen it), but it is available on DVD and blu-ray 3D.

(2013) *The Great Martian War 1913 - 1917* Clearly resetting the dates of the Martian invasion to present an alternate history of World War I in which real events of the 'Great War' are woven into events from the novel. The film was originally presented in the UK on December 8, 2013 as the World War One centennial approached. A deliberate attempt to approach history through the Martian invasion, this combination of archival footage and CGI effects was found to be 'interesting' by some reviewers and 'gripping,' even 'awesome' by others.

It is available on DVD.

Acknowledgements: "You gotta see these!"

In composing a survey of unmade films, it is impossible to move forward without 'standing on the shoulders of giants.' The following works were essential and are recommended.

KEEP WATCHING THE SKIES! THE 21ST CENTURY EDITION (Bill Warren McFarland Books 2010) The late Bill Warren's book is essential reading for any science fiction movie fan, and its immaculately researched entries frequently detail unmade versions of films and alternate ideas lost on the way to production. I wish Bill had done a book like this for the 1960s and 1970s before he passed, but he left that very consciously for others to do because he thought the author should be someone who experienced the movies in their 'sense of wonder' years. Come on guys - it's time (and maybe time for a book on the 80's too). Beg, borrow, or steal a copy.

HARRYHAUSEN THE LOST MOVIES (John Walsh and the Ray and Diana Harryhausen Foundation Titan Books 2019) This is a magnificent collection of artwork and images of test footage from the unmade films of Ray Harryhausen. Although I have some problems with some of the supporting text (John Walsh seems unaware that the appearance of wires supporting the martian ships in Pal's The War of the Worlds is an artifact of the film's VHS/DVD aging Eastmancolor transfers and not present in the original Technicolor prints) overall it is a beautiful record of an enduring artist's behind-the-scenes work.

WAR OF THE WORLDS: FROM WELLS TO SPIELBERG (John L. Flynn, PH.D. Galactic Books 2nd edition 2019) Science Fiction writer and English professor John L. Flynn has created an excellent overview of all things War of the Worlds from the novel to the radio play to the film and later television series production. He covers Jeff Wayne's musical version as well, and films inspired by the story. A great book for 'martian-completists.'

SCIENCE FICTION TELEVISION SERIES (2 volumes) (Mark Phillips and Frank Garcia McFarland Books 2006) The two authors have written for Cinefantastique, Starlog, Film Fax and many other SF media publications over the years. While the book focuses on casts and credits for 62 prime time shows from 1959 to 1989, the interviews and histories that lead each entry are fascinating. Again, recommended for the obsessed.

LEE POWERS REVIEWS!

Previously on LEE POWERS REVIEWS, Lee reviewed the 1959 kaiju flick from the Philippines called ANAK NG BULKAN, today he returns to review the 1997 remake.

The story starts off with a native boy named Pedirin who is being taught by his stepfather to hunt boars along with another boy, Adam, who is friends with Pedirin. The three of them succeed in obtaining a boar and head back to the village. A journalist named CJ arrives by plane at the airport looking for a new story at the same time. Meanwhile, Pedirin arrives home and tells his mother about his adventure hunting the boar. Suddenly, Pedirin's step father violently grabs him by the ears and berates him for not selling the illegal cigarettes that he gave him. He also forbids him from hanging out with the natives and listening to their silly stories of a mystical volcano bird...

Later that evening, Pedirin tells his mother that the beatings don't bother him anymore, but still wishes his real father was there. After this we return to the reporter, CJ, who is visiting with a priest, Father O'Reilly. She is looking for leads on a story, and he gives her a few topics to look into, notably the volcano.

The next day, Pedirin comes running out of the jungle to tell his mother that the natives are predicting the volcano to erupt soon. His stepfather just laughs and shrugs it off, claiming that it won't happen. However, as predicted, the volcano erupts while CJ and her crew film it. Within some of the flowing hot lava and mud is a large egg. Pedirin and his friend, Leslie, find it just as it cracks open to reveal a baby Pterodactyl. (That said, in the whole film it is only identified as a bird despite its dinosaurian appearance.) The boy explains to Leslie it is Vulcan, the mountain god the natives were telling him about. Pedirin and Leslie take Vulcan (Balkan in the original language) to the village to hide him in a chicken coop, where it fights with the roosters.

CJ, back with Father O'Reilly, thanks him for the leads and offers to donate some money to his ministry. Father O'Reilly then asks CJ to investigate a military officer named captain Cody Jennings, who went missing and left behind a young boy and his mother in the Philippines. CJ agrees to do so. (You can see where this is going...)

Meanwhile, Vulcan has grown much larger in only one day. Having outgrown the chicken coop, Pedirin and Leslie take Vulcan back to the cave where they found him. The natives surround the children and accuse them of stealing their god. Pedirin explains what happened and the natives begin to understand that the boy rescued the animal, and so then regard Pedirin as Vulcan's guardian.

After this, Pedirin goes for a ride on Vulcan and is observed by the natives. Vulcan also flies over some neighboring villages and is filmed by CJ. Later, her report is shown on local television stations. (By now Vulcan is a little smaller than the giant condor from *Godzilla vs. the Sea Monster* [1966], and it remains this size for duration of the film.) A poacher notices Vulcan on TV and decides to capture him in an effort to pay a debt he owes to a tyrant businessman. (Vernon Wells plays the villain, and also appeared in Arnold Schwarzenegger's *Commando* [1985]. The businessman is none other than Robert Vaughn!)

The next day, Pedirin's stepdad is suspiciously nice to him, promising him in front of his mother that they'll be a better family. However, later when he and Pedirin are alone he threatens him with more abuse if he doesn't hand over the bird so he can sell it, then proceeds to slap him around.

Vulcan comes to rescue him and lets out a loud roar (which sounds like a combination of a lion and King Kong.) Vulcan chases the abusive stepfather away and sprays a stream of fire onto his backside setting his pants on fire!!! Vulcan then lets out a bellow-like laugh.

Meanwhile, CJ finds out that Pedirin's real father was killed in action while in the Marines and was a war hero. Elsewhere, the poacher tracks Vulcan and the children and manages to capture them. The volcano then erupts again, with lava and molten mud raining down on small towns and villages. CJ manages to thwart the poacher's sale of Vulcan to a scientist, and the children escape to free the monster bird. Pedirin and Vulcan then fly around to rescue villagers that need to escape the lava. But, the poacher is on the loose again and ready to kill Vulcan. Pedirin begs Vulcan to return to the volcano to escape being killed by the poacher.

The tyrant businessman (remember him, the one that the poacher owes money to?) catches up to the poacher and kills him to settle his debt, inadvertently saving the day. Vulcan then flies back to the mountain as Pedirin and the natives happily wave goodbye.

Overall, the *Anak Ng Bulkan* remake presents lighthearted entertainment in the vein of *The Adventures of Galgameth* (1997). As for the special effects, the Vulcan pterodactyl is a few notches below Rodan as he appeared in *Godzilla vs. Mechagodzilla* (1993) but still looks pretty good. I purchased this film on VHS a long time ago, and as there is no DVD release as of yet, so that's the only way you can see it.

TEENAGE MUTANT NINJA TURTLES IV: THE NEXT MUTATION

In 1990, *Teenage Mutant Ninja Turtles* became the highest grossing independent movie of all time. It was followed by two sequels that saw diminishing returns, with *Teenage Mutant Ninja Turtles III* only grossing $42 million. Even though it was considered a disappointment, New Line still asked *Turtles* creators Kevin Eastman and Peter Laird to start working on a fourth film. And why would they do that if the last film bombed? Because the VHS sales were still relatively good, and tie in toy sales were still very good.

And, to that end, what Eastman and Laird essentially did was design what would make for cool new action figures for the Turtles. As it is, there really aren't any solid story ideas for what was called *Teenage Mutant Ninja Turtles IV: The Next Mutation*—only lots of concept art. (And, I don't know about the prospective movie itself, but the toys that would have resulted from it would have been awesome!)

In my own humble opinion, I would guess that the story was written around the designs rather than the designs being a product of the plot. What little story we do know of centered around the turtles growing past their teenage stage, and when they do, the mutagen in their blood mutates further, giving each turtle (and Splinter) distinct new abilities. At the same time, new villains show up in New York looking to fill the power void left by Shredder. Actually, that last sentence might have been part of a different *TMNT IV*... unfortunately all iterations of the fourth film tend to get blended together. (We'll talk about another abandoned concept a bit later.)

But, back to the basic history of *Next Mutation*: From the best that experts have been able to put together, the fourth live action turtle movie was in development from 1994 until late 1997 when it was finally abandoned. Most of *Turtle* fandom first learned of the project via Peter Laird's Blast from the Past blog series in the early 2000s. For fun, he began posting images of the turtle's redesigns from *The Next Mutation* movie. To call the new designs interesting would be an understatement. As stated before, all the turtles would be given new powers/looks thanks to the titular "Next Mutation."

Leonardo would have gained impenetrable skin of some type. Laird wrote, "I believe Leo's new mutation was the ability to morph his skin into a kind of nearly impenetrable chrome-like surface (shades of Ben Boxer from Jack Kirby's 'Kamandi' comics!)." As to his new design, Laird said, "The 'rising sun' bandana on Leo in this version actually comes from a much earlier costume redesign session, when we were toying around with changing the costumes for the Turtles in the comic books. I kind of dig the 'utility belt' Leo has in this drawing."

"Don was given the least obvious mutation -- growing telekinetic and telepathic abilities, unfortunately counterpointed by diminishing eyesight (hence the vision-enhancing goggles)," Laird said of Donatello. "We also provided him with an updated 'techno' version of his bo staff." The diminishing eye sight idea, it seems, was cooked up just as an excuse to make Don wear the goggles! Poor Donatello.

Since Michelangelo was the most human-like of the bunch in terms of his personality, he was given an ability to tie in with that. In this case, he would somehow be able to change his appearance to look like a human being. "Here we gave Mike a more 'street' look because his new mutation gave him the ability to project a human appearance onto his turtle features, allowing him to interact freely with humans." In another comment Laird reflected that,

"This reminds me a little of an even earlier idea Kevin and I toyed with for the *TMNT* comics. We had this (admittedly more than a bit goofy) plan to have Donatello make 'human disguises' which the Turtles could wear that would allow them to move around undetected in public. These disguises would not have survived really close examination, though... for example, to accommodate the Turtles' three-fingered hands, they would wear special latex gloves which from a distance would look like human five-fingered hands, but actually had the index finger and middle finger fused into one, and the other two fingers also fused together in this way. I think I have a quick sketch of this somewhere, but I haven't seen it in a while."

And then there was Raphael, which has become the best known of the *Next Mutation* bunch. He would've been mutated into a type of dinosaur-turtle! "One of our ideas was to give Raphael the ability to 'morph' into what we were calling 'Raptor Raph', complete with big gnashy teeth and claws to complement his

big gnashy personality." Don't forget, *Jurassic Park* had just been released, and the raptors pretty much stole the show, so it was no wonder that out of all the dinosaurs to morph Raph into, they chose the Raptor.

Similar to the gimmick given to Raphael was the one given to Splinter. I suppose one could have called this the Super Splinter à la Super Shredder. "We wanted to give Splinter a much more active part in the battles that the Turtles fought, and so he was going to have the ability to morph into a big, lithe, muscular 'super rat mutant' type of thing." Though the design is undeniably cool, and seeing Splinter fight in the films was always a highlight, part of what made Splinter so fun was that he could still fight in spite of his advanced age. This new power would have taken away from that aspect of the character, even though it does look amazing.

And then there's Kirby, the fifth turtle. Although numerous drawings of him exist dating back to 1994, we're not actually sure he was slated to be in *Next Mutation*. We're also not sure of his function in the story. Was he a long lost brother? Was he a brand new turtle mutant like Rahzar from *TMNT II*? Was he even friend or foe? We don't know, but most fans hedge their bets on him starting out as a foe and turning into an ally by the film's ending.

But, here's what we do know about Kirby. First off, he was named after Jack Kirby, and would have had four fingers instead of three and would have used butterfly knives as his signature weapons. In some concept art, he has a white bandana to set him apart better from his brethren. He also has tiger stripes on his skin in many drawings. In another more sinister-looking version of the character, he has a black bandana. Yet another has him wearing a pinkish purple purple bandana along with a cape.

Prior to Lair's blog posts, the first "hard evidence" for the film's production came from *CBS Action Zone* #1, a comic book produced by CBS to promote their Saturday Morning Cartoon lineup. This 1994 debut issue featured an image of "Raptor Raph" in it. It didn't name the project, as you can see to the right, but it did contain the image of Raph at least.

The project was still being talked about in comics in 1996, specifically in the letters section of Image's *TMNT Volume 3* which claimed that the movie was "in the works."

That same year, the film was teased in the 1996 Playmates Toys catalog, which had a full-page advertisement for *TMNT IV* (bottom right). Notably it featured a teaser silhouette for Kirby drawn by Michael Dooney and also identified Trimark Pictures as the producer, not Mirage Entertainment. However, the text betrays the original plot outline given by Lair in his blog, as the catalog stated, "Look out for the fourth and hottest Turtle feature film ever! It's a weird world of parallel dimensions and gothic proportions - and Playmates is backing it all the way with a multi-million dollar promotional campaign and a massive mound of Mutant movie Turtle toys!"

As you just read, there was no mention of new mutations, but instead parallel dimensions. Furthermore, the catalog alluded to the film being a late 1996 release. Among the figures advertised was a Cyber Kirby, though this may not necessarily hint at any plot points, as Playmates often did weird offshoots of the turtles just to sell more toys.

Form the best that I can piece together, by this time the subtitle of *The Next Mutation* had been re-

placed by a new one: *The Foot Walks Again*. We know about this title due to an auction that sold off *TMNT* memorabilia from Kevin Eastman, including three scripts related to the fourth unmade movie in 2012. The scripts are dated January 27, 1995 (with Christian Ford and Roger Soffer as the writers); the second is simply dated 1996 (a rewrite of the previous script by Craig Shapiro and John Travis); and then the final draft is dated July of 1997, again by Shapiro and Travis.

This one has a clearer story concept, where the Turtles would somehow get sucked into an alternate dimension where they would come across new villains, plus what look to be evil versions of April and "Kasey" (yes, the parallel world version is spelled with a 'K'). This is also where they would meet Kirby. Going off of the concept art, there appears to be a scene of "evil April" trying to help the turtles pull Kirby through a portal to rescue him, which means regardless of how they began the story, it looks like the parallel earth April and Kirby would end up as good guys in the end.

As for other details, the Foot Clan used guns in this parallel world. Numerous new villains were pitched, but the one that stuck was named Spyder. And, there was a new Super Shredder! "Shredder got put back together with nanobots," Eastman said on the PJ and Pals Podcast in 2019.

Lucky for us, Eastman commented at length on the project again elsewhere:

"I was doing most of the traveling for the company at this point and began regular trips to Los Angeles to work with the writers, and run the progress back to Mirage HQ In Northampton, Massachusetts. After

TMNT MOVIE FOUR

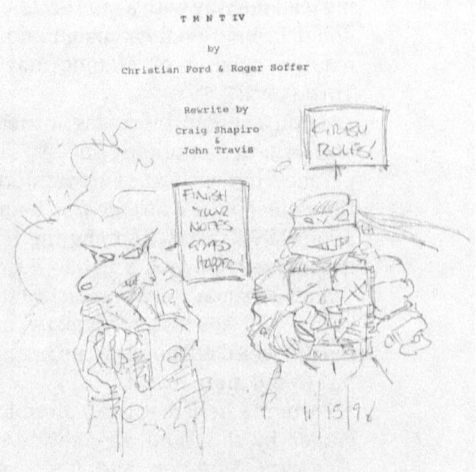

two drafts were completed, New Line abandoned the project-and a year later Motion Picture Corporation of America optioned the rights, and I continued to work on behalf of Mirage Studios developing the ideas for the picture - and as with the original New Line draft, this version also featured a fifth TMNT character we would introduce - named after our main inspiration/hero Jack 'King' Kirby."

Unfortunately, the contents of the screenplays sold in the 2012 auction have never been fully revealed. All we know are the dates, and that the project came to an end in 1997. Perhaps not coincidentally, 1997 saw the release of a new live action TV series: *Ninja Turtles: The Next Mutation*. And, in addition to repurposing the *Next Mutation* subtitle, it also introduced a fifth turtle... but it wasn't Kirby. Instead it was a female turtle named Venus de Milo that was universally reviled by fans. (I personally thought the idea of a female turtle sounded cool, but, by the time that series premiered I had lost interest in the turtles and never watched it.) Before this, in 1995, the 9th season of the original cartoon series also had all four turtles mutate into Raptor turtles during their unstable mutation arc. Then, in the 2003 series, Donatello turned into a turtle Raptor! So at least that idea was used a couple of times.

Overall, it's debatable just how a fourth live action *TMNT* movie would have fared, and in any case, it's sad that the series went out with a whimper rather than a bang via 1993's poorly received *Teenage Mutant Ninja Turtles III*. As I said before, I have a funny feeling *TMNT IV* wouldn't have been a great movie, but I think it would have resulted in some great toys, that's for sure!

KING OF TERROR
KING GHIDORAH FLIES SOLO

In 1995, before the imminent death of Godzilla in *Godzilla vs. Desotroyah* would even take place on theater screens, Toho was already thinking of how to supplant the King of the Monsters. To do so, they talked of spin-off movies for the Queen of the Monsters and the King of Terror. This is, of course, Mothra and King Ghidorah. It was thought that the Mothra spinoff would come out first, and the King Ghidorah spinoff would come out in 1998, to take advantage of the doomsday hype surrounding 1999 (that said, it could have been eyed for December of 1999, too). Unfortunately, no story details have ever been revealed outside of Ghidorah being an alien King of Terror that appears in 1999. In an abstract way, this project was completed as *Mothra 3: Invasion of King Ghidorah* (1998). But, had it been a Ghidorah solo movie, what could we have expected? The answer might lay in an old treatment from Shinji Nishikawa, meant as a competing story concept against Kazuki Omori's version of *Godzilla vs. King Ghidorah* (Nishikawa turned in his pitch on January 14, 1991, while Omori had already done two different versions of what would become *Godzilla vs. King Ghidorah*).

Like the unmade *Godzilla: Legend of the Asuka Fortress*, this movie would be set in the future rather than having people from the future serve as villains. Specifically, the story is set in the 23rd Century (yes the same era the Futurians hail from) where observatories track a strange asteroid that emits powerful electromagnetic waves heading straight for Earth. To investigate, the exploration ship "Shiratori" is launched to rendezvous with the celestial body near Neptune's orbit. The asteroid has a maximum diameter of less than 100 meters. The celestial body suddenly emits a flash of bright light, and begins to generate a strong magnetic force -- obviously a callback to the magnetic meteor from *Ghidorah, the Three Headed Monster* (1964). What happens next might be a callback to

Gorath (1962), as the "Shiratori" is drawn in by the magnetic force and is destroyed.

Shades of *Gorath* continue as the mysterious asteroid continues to hurtle towards Earth undaunted, even after missiles strike it in an attempt to change its trajectory. Instead the alien orb increases its speed! A powerful futuristic space fleet is launched to battle the alien object near Jupiter. The idea is to knock it into Jupiter's immense gravity, and hope that the asteroid will be drawn into it. The plan seems to work, and down the asteroid goes into a cloud of methane. As everyone celebrates, the orb levitates out of Jupiter's atmosphere. At that point the experts realize it has anti-gravity properties. The space fleet attacks again, and the asteroid is engulfed in flames... you know where this is going.

The ball of fire turns an even brighter red and three pillars of fire are expelled from the orb. The three pillars are in fact the necks of a dragon that begins to form. Feet, tails, and wings also materialize from the flames. King Ghidorah makes short work of the space fleet and makes a course for Earth.

Nishikawa ends his pitch, which is really just a tease for the main story, with some exposition about how King Ghidorah returns to earth every 26 million years to cause an extinction level event (so yes, like the King Ghidorah in *Mothra 3*, this version of the character eradicated the dinosaurs). The last line in Nishikawa's treatment goes, "The battle between the Defense Forces and King Ghidorah for humanity's survival is about to begin, and a black shadow is now moving deep under the sea."

This black shadow is obviously Godzilla. In fact, this treatment had me excited until that line, because for a moment I thought perhaps that this was an outline for the abandoned King Ghidorah solo vehicle pondered in 1995. All we know about the Ghidorah film was that it would have the monster descend from the stars as the fulfilment of Nostradamus's "King of Terror" prophecy in the year 1999. Toho had a longstanding fascination with this concept, dating back to 1975's unmade *Great Prophecies of Nostradamus II: King of Terror*. (In that case, the "King of Terror" would be what turns out to be a UFO that is benevolent to the Japanese peoples as the rest of the world self destructs).

Though Nishikawa's treatment was just a teaser to the battle between Godzilla and Ghidorah, I wouldn't doubt it that this treatment was looked at in terms of the Ghidorah solo vehicle in 1995. Though this could be a coincidence, *Mothra 3* did use an idea from this treatment, that being that King Ghidorah killed the dinosaurs. Let's not forget that *Mothra 3* originally had the big bug traveling back in time not to the days of the dinosaurs, but to Feudal Japan a la *Teenage Mutant Ninja Turtles 3*. There Mothra would have battled a fire monster. Toho could have simply supplanted the fire monster with Ghidorah and kept the story set in Edo, but they changed it to the Cretaceous. I think this was due to Nishikawa's treatment. Besides, it wasn't unusual for Toho to look through old treatments for ideas (the idea of Godzilla having a nuclear meltdown dates back to 1991, or possibly even a 1985 entry into the *Godzilla 2* contest).

So, bottom line, had the King Ghidorah solo movie gone forth, I think it would've started out a lot like this treatment... just, ya know, without Godzilla in it.

THE LOST FILMS FANZINE #5 SPRING 2021

WHAT HAPPENED TO THE BIG STUFFED DOG THAT CAME TO NBC???

By Matthew B. Lamont

It is well known that the prolific Charles M. Schultz wrote the Peanuts stories, where he used his childhood experiences and channeled it in his works. All the creative talent was put into his comics, cartoons, and feature films. The first NBC Peanuts-related project was *You're a Good Man Charlie Brown* (1973). This was an episode of the anthology series Hallmark Hall of Fame. A second one, which is what we are going to take a deep look at, came out on February 8, 1981 as part of NBC's Project Peacock, which was a series of TV specials aimed for family viewing. It was called *The Big Stuffed Dog* and was a Lee Mendelson and Charles M. Schultz production (Schultz also wrote the film as well). Brace yourself, as you will laugh, you will cry, and you will end up wondering why.

The story begins with a boy named Petey (Rossie Harris) going to his grandfather's farm for two weeks and he brings his large Snoopy doll with him. His father (Robert Ginty) doesn't approve of it, but his mother is OK with it. At the airport, the doll gets a lot of attention from people and even pet dogs. Although Petey's mother has two tickets for the flight to Stafford Chapel, a businessman (Arthur Rosenberg) needs a seat on the plane. As a solution, the ticket agent suggests that the plush pooch should be put in the animal carrier. They all agree and Petey puts it in the luggage carrier and this is where the adventure begins.

At the Stafford Chapel airport, two bikers led by Crazy (Gordon Jump of *WKRP in Cincinnati* fame) and his large friend Link (Michael Pritchard) are waiting for a stuffed animal with money inside. Out comes Snoopy

50

from the baggage claim and the bikers go off with the title doll. Little do they know, the money is in a stuffed raccoon doll wearing overalls. The silly bikers ride off with the big beagle strapped to the seat, but the straps break and it falls down some stairs, crashing into some trash cans. Back at the airport, Petey arrives, meets his grandfather (Noah Beery Jr. of *The Rockford Files*), picks up his bag, but finds his beloved stuffed dog gone.

Back in the city, a lonely old woman (Mildred Dunnock of *Baby Doll* fame) finds the dog and takes him home, leading to the saddest part of the special. At her home, she talks to him as if he were a real visitor. She speaks about the marbles, the collection of Big Little Books (which were very popular from 1930s to 1960s), and the tragedies of being old. The following day, her grandson (David-James Carroll) comes to visit her, but Superintendent Browder (Mel Stewart of *In the Heat of the Night*) says that she died in her sleep, so a sale is being held. At the sale, a yellow car appears and out steps an amusement park worker (Abe Vigoda of *The Godfather* notoriety), who buys the dog for $10 (and comically struggles to get it in his car) and drives off. Shortly after, the motorcycle gang comes to the sale, and Crazy asks if they have seen the dog. The superintendent tells him that it was sold to the man in the Volkswagen, and off they go after him.

Next we meet a girl named Lily at her home, (Sydney Penny, who would later voice Lucy in the animated special, *It's Magic Charlie Brown*). She is instructing her friend Robbie James (Robbie Kiger) how to make small balloons so that she can practice throwing darts at them for her big day at the carnival. There, the barker has hung up his recently purchased Snoopy doll. Lily and Robby arrive at the balloon popping stand and Lily really wants to win the dog. The carnival barker says that if she wants it, she has to pop 60 balloons. After Lily accomplishes the challenge, the barker doesn't want to give her the dog. This leads him to give her one last challenge: popping an incredibly tiny yellow balloon. If she pops it, she will get the dog and tickets to all the rides. She wins and takes the prized pooch on various rides. After this, she notices that the dog's nose is starting to come off, and decides to take it to the hospital.

At the hospital, a nurse (Denise Nicholas of *Room 222*) takes notice of a fretful child, worried about having his tonsils being removed. She asks Lily about her Snoopy doll and its nose, which seems to be coming off. The nurse has an idea to show the boy scheduled for the tonsillectomy a doctor (Tom Dahlgren of *Invasion of the Body Snatchers* [1978]) sewing the plush dog's nose back on. The trick works like a charm, and the boy becomes less nervous for his surgery.

Meanwhile, Petey asks his grandfather to call his parents to see if they have found his cuddly canine. But, when grandfather calls, no one answers. That night, as Lily is walking home from the hospital with the dog, some friendly police officers ask her if she needs a ride home. She declines the offer, which turns out to be a mistake. Wouldn't you know it, a little later the bikers see the dog, and a chase begins. Lily hides the stuffed animal in a large basket in a dark area and runs to safety.

The next day, we learn that the basket is actually the carriage of a hot air balloon, rented out for a ride by newlyweds! After the minister (Scott Beach) pronounces them as husband and wife, up they go and find the massive plush pooch. The groom (Terry David Mulligan) wants to throw him out, but the bride (Debbie Miller) wants him to stay, and so he does. After some lovely wide shots of the landscape, Petey and his grandfather just happen to be fishing when they spot the balloon. Petey can see his missing pet plush toy, which unexpectedly (read: conveniently) falls from the balloon and into the water. Petey's grandfather fishes it out and into the boat, where Petey happily reunites with his pooch.

At the same time, at the carnival, Link, one of the bikers, reads a newspaper article about the real stuffed doll that they were looking for, (you know, the raccoon?). It has been found by a man who subsequently gave it to his son and discovered a $100 bill within the doll's broken seam! Lily approaches the bikers and asks about last night's chase. Crazy explains that they meant her no harm were simply after the dog, leading to an apology. Lily then tells them that throwing darts at balloons is the best way to get a big stuffed plush doll. Crazy likes the idea, but the other bikers become disgusted and leave. The End.

Good grief! Is this a Peanuts Special like the VHS tape from 1996 claimed? No, not at all. It can only be a Peanuts Special if it was animated, and contained characters

From Top Left: Title Card; the bikers at the airport; Lily with the Snoopy plush on a rollercoaster; the doll takes a hot air balloon ride; and Petey reunites with his doll.

like Charlie Brown, Snoopy, Woodstock, Lucy, Linus, Sally, Schroder, Marcie and Peppermint Patty. There was a Snoopy doll in it, yes, but that doesn't really qualify as the canine cartoon character. That said, it does feel like a live-action Peanuts special since it was written Schultz. The scene at the airport gave a vibe that was reminiscent of the cartoons.

As for the characters, Lily was like a live-action version of Lucy Van Pelt with her tough attitude and her interaction with Robbie James (it is no wonder she took the part of Lucy in

What makes this feel like a live-action Peanuts special is the music by Ed Bogas and Judy Munsen. Lily's theme has a slow electric guitar similar to those used in specials like *You're The Greatest Charlie Brown* (1979). The bikers' theme song sounds like upbeat, happy, big band music similar to *Happy New Year Charlie Brown* (1986). Even the sad moments, like the lonely old lady scene, and intense ones (like the title doll's nose getting stitched back) sounded like something you would hear from those cartoons (closest to 1980's *Life is a Circus Charlie Brown*).

And, the strangest thing about this special: It was directed by Robert Fuest. Yes, the same man who directed *The Abominable Dr. Phibes* (1971) and *Dr. Phibes Rides Again* (1972)! This film doesn't feel like any of his previous movies, so perhaps he was a director for hire. Or, maybe, he was secretly a Peanuts fan and watched the animated specials with his kids, or read the comics as a source of distraction?

In any case, you won't find this special on DVD, you won't find it on Blu-Ray,

It's Magic Charlie Brown). Petey is similar to Charlie Brown or Linus, who loves his stuffed doll, just like Linus with his blanket or Charlie Brown with Snoopy. The silly motorcycle gang are like adult versions of the goofy bullies from the film *Race for Your Life Charlie Brown* (1977), except in the end, they weren't really bad guys at all.

and you won't find it on any streaming service. It can only be found wherever OOP VHS tapes are sold, and the World Wide Web (ie, the Internet). Happy hunting to true blue Charlie Brown and Snoopy fans, as this special will likely only appeal to them.

GRIZZLY II UNLEASHED

Today, after nearly forty years of waiting, I finally saw *Grizzly II*, that most mythic of unfinished films. Well, I guess I've only been waiting two years (that's how long I've been aware of its existence). Plus, it started shooting a few years before I was born, so my math was wrong on several counts. But, the point is, it's a momentous occasion. It's a rare instance of a film that was only partially shot and then abandoned to later be resurrected, edited, completed, and released close to forty years later. Was I blown away by what I saw? In some ways, yes. In others, no. But, above all else, I want to say I have nothing but respect for producer Suzanne Nagy for taking over the film when it was abandoned and seeing to it that it got done.

Before we go any further, a few of you might be asking what the big deal is with *Grizzly II*. If you know, you can probably skip the next few paragraphs, but if you don't, prepare to be enlightened.

First off, in case you couldn't tell by the title, the film is a sequel to *Grizzly*, a *Jaws* knock off (and a damn good one at that) released in 1976. It was a huge hit, which naturally meant a sequel would be produced. The story was written by original *Grizzly* writer David Sheldon and his actress wife, Joan McCall. Eventually producer Joseph Proctor approached Sheldon about his script, and Sheldon agreed to give it to him on the condition that he got to direct. That didn't happen.

Sheldon got swindled out of the director's chair due to difficulties securing a suitable filming location in the U.S. The problem was that the centerpiece of the movie was a rock concert held in the middle of Yellowstone National Forest. Proctor, knowing that filming a rock concert would be near impossible due to shooting restrictions in the U.S., decided he would fare better by shooting the entire picture overseas. Suzanne C. Nagy, a Hungarian economist, was brought on as a producer on the tentatively titled *Grizzly II: The Concert*.

To film the all-important concert scene a Russian military base was secured as the venue. Instead of simply recreating a rock concert like a normal film would do, the producers staged a real rock concert, even charging the "extras" $15 per ticket to attend! The concert was marketed as a three-day event, and 50,000 people ended up attending. The rock concert, by the way, doesn't look the least bit American and screams Euro-rock.

But the misplaced rock concert might have been the least of the film's problems. This time, there was no trained bear as was the case on the last film. Instead, all the main bear scenes would be accomplished via animatronics and "a guy in a bear suit." Reportedly, the animatronic rarely worked, and the bear suit looked terrible. This, and other problems, necessitated some rewrites. And who did they get to rewrite the script? Well, they couldn't get Sheldon as Proctor had already screwed him out of the director's chair, and so the on-set caterer was hired to do the rewrites. Why? Well, that we don't know, but presumably there was some reason behind it.

And, even before the mishaps with the mechanical bear, Proctor disappeared from the production along with most of the film's money. In a 2014 interview, Proctor denied that he took the funds. Proctor told the interviewer this from his jail cell at the Los Angeles Federal Prison, where he was carrying out a five-

Don't let the bear fool you, John Rhys-Davies is the star of the show as Bouchard! GRIZZLY II © GBGB International

year sentence for tax evasion.

I had always assumed Proctor's departure came about midway through the shoot, but according to Nagy on the official *Grizzly II* website, it happened after the concert was shot! According to Nagy, "The first day of shooting was the most important event—a Woodstock-style concert where a gigantic grizzly bear attacks people. It was a fantastic and mesmerizing day. Everything worked out– the weather, the rock bands, the 40,000 audience."

Nagy continued to explain how shocked she was when Proctor left with the funds, and how she then had to refinance the movie and finish the 45 day shoot herself. Quite a feat for the producer! Nagy managed to finish most of the principal photography, but as stated earlier, the effects footage with the bear was apparently deemed unusable in the end. Sadly, there was no money left to finish the special effects scenes by this time. Adding to the troubles was the fact that Proctor wouldn't relinquish his rights on the film until four years later. Free of Proctor, Nagy made a deal with Cannon Films in 1987 to finish the movie. It was more bad luck for Nagy, as Cannon found themselves in financial troubles and would fold a few years later.

And, for twenty plus years, the *Grizzly II* footage sat in a Paris film lab, while the soundtrack was located in a vault in New York. A workprint of the film was screened in 2007. The bear itself only appeared during the end concert scenes, and preceding this, scenes featuring the bear consisted of a blank screen. Then, after years of sitting in the vault, in 2018 Nagy decided to finish the film once and for all.

And the review starts here... so ya know, spoilers, yada yada, you've been warned.

Above: Laura Dern and George Clooney as doomed lovers. Right: Charlie Scheen as one of the other doomed teens. GRIZZLY II © GBGB International

Grizzly II: Revenge is a tough film to judge under the circumstances. The movie is quite short at only 75 minutes (because the film never actually finished shooting). If I had to guess, I'd estimate the movie was probably supposed to run at least 90-100 minutes. Sadly, Nagy was left with what I would calculate to be about one hour's worth of usable footage. Said footage comprised of incomplete scenes, lacking alternate angles for the actors, pick-up shots, things like that. You can tell by the dialogue that little snippets to bridge the footage here and there oftentimes either wasn't available or was never shot to begin with. And, considering that all the actors still living have aged forty years, there was no way to do reshoots. Or, I suppose what I'm trying to say is, I do not envy the editor of this film. As such, *Grizzly II* is a hybrid between footage clearly from the 1980s and new insert shots from today.

One scene that definitely went unfilmed was the opening, where the mother Grizzly and her cub were to be shot by a hunter, which kicks off the story about a mother Grizzly (who just happens to be twenty feet tall) out to avenge her cubs. This sequence is recreated and is well done except it's clearly very new footage (I wish they could have aged the new footage to make it match the original better). After this pre-credits scene, mega stars George Clooney, Charlie Sheen and Laura Dern are credited first, which was off putting to me initially. The trio is barely in the movie -- all they are is a group of disposable teenagers killed by the bear. However, they also end up being

GRIZZLY II's giant mama bear looks pretty good for an 80s animatronic.
GRIZZLY II © GBGB International

the very first actors that we see—so there's that at least (first credited, first seen, fair enough). That said, they are slaughtered soon after their introduction.

One thing that interests me about *Grizzly II* is that it was even more like *Jaws* than *Grizzly* was. It also reminded me of the *Jaws* sequels. For instance, like the shark in *Jaws 2*, the bear in *Grizzly II* is a bigger, female bear (*Jaws 2's* shark was also female, in case you didn't know). Furthermore, the monsters both meet their ends in similar fashions via electrocution. On another note, *Jaws 3-D* was released in 1983, the year this film was shot. I don't think that *Jaws 3-D* could have influenced *Grizzly II*, because if I'm not mistaken *Grizzly II* was shot first. That said, they have similarities also. Both are slightly more high-concept than their predecessors. For instance, in *Jaws* and *Grizzly* the threat looms over the summer tourist season in general. In *Jaws 3-D* there is a specific event for the monster to wreak (the opening of a new Sea World attraction) and in *Grizzly II* it is a huge outdoor con-

THE LOST FILMS FANZINE #5 SPRING 2021

GRIZZLY II © GBGB International

cert. Also, both films hinge upon a mother predator out to avenge her dead offspring.

Grizzly's character structure slightly mirrored *Jaws*, but *Grizzly II* does even more so. If you'll recall the archetypes of Brody, Hooper, and Quint in *Jaws*, here the head park ranger, Nick Hollister (Steve Inwood), is clearly Brody. Then there's the hunter, Bouchard (John Rhys-Davies), who with his thick accent and gruff demeanor is clearly Quint. (Bouchard is by and large the star of the show, even above the bear. He's just too interesting!) Lastly there is Dr. Samantha Owens (Deborah Raffin), the Quint stand-in. Owens and Bouchard argue about the bear, which she wants to tranquilize and relocate, while he only wants to kill it. Owens isn't necessarily wrong, the poor bear is wounded and bereaved, it wasn't violent by nature. But, then again, Bouchard isn't wrong either, as the bear is a threat to innocent human lives. And this is exactly why their scenes together are so interesting. Sadly, we never really get to see those two characters bond or reconcile like we did Hooper and Quint, and I have a feeling it's because shooting ended prematurely.

As for the bear, like the shark in the first *Jaws*, we don't really see it until the very end. Before that, it's mostly seen via very quick snippets. This wasn't an artistic decision though, it was just a stroke of luck that the bear footage was actually filmed for the climax. And what we do see of the bear looks great for the time, in my opinion at least.

There's some pretty good gore scenes that should please fans of animals attack movies. For instance, an unlikable hunter is found impaled high above the ground on a tree branch. Bouchard himself dies by impalement on the concert scaffolding by the bear. (However, I bet had there been a *Grizzly III* he would've come back, he doesn't look that dead...)

The film ends on a high note, even if it is tonally inconsistent. If anything, I would compare the film's last moment to *The Lost Boys*, where it's revealed that grandpa knew there were vampires in Santa Carla the entire time but never bothered to tell his family about it. Here, the bear does indeed interrupt the live concert. Hollister (the ranger) lures it in front of an electrified fence and it gets fried in front of the horrified concert goers as well as a politician in the company of the park superintendent. "Is that part of the show?" the politician asks. The superintendant, who knows good and damn well that it's not (she was warned profusely about the bear and ignored it) pauses for a moment, then answers, "Yes. Yes, it is." They sit back down, and we cut to the credits. It's hilarious, intentionally hilarious just to be clear, but is also tonally inconsistent considering there were no other jokes in the film.

Again, my hat is off to the producer and editor under the circumstances in terms of working with what they had. I can tell that had the film been able to finish shooting in its original era it would be well remembered today. (I have no doubt that *Jaws* rip-off fans would all be quoting Bouchard's character on the regular!) I truly regret that we can't see the film as originally intended, because a good 80s monster movie is definitely in there! But, I also rejoice that Nagy and her crew put in the hard work to finish the film which is something that all of we lost films aficionados should be thankful for.

If I were to lodge one complaint against the film, which I don't think is justified, is that I wish the music and title graphics could have looked more era appropriate. However, there wasn't much money to put into finishing the picture, evident by stock music comprising parts of the score (there is one synthesized, 80s appropriate track that occurs when Dr. Owens is getting chased by a bear). That little grievance aside, I still hope that the producers make so much money off of the DVD sales that perhaps one day they can come back and do another cut of the film with a different soundtrack and better titles that look era appropriate. (And maybe something to age the new footage?)

So, even though it's not perfect, I still highly recommend *Grizzly II* to fans of the Animals Attack genre as well as film historians. The film can be rented digitally or bought on Blu-Ray from Amazon.com and many other major retailers.

 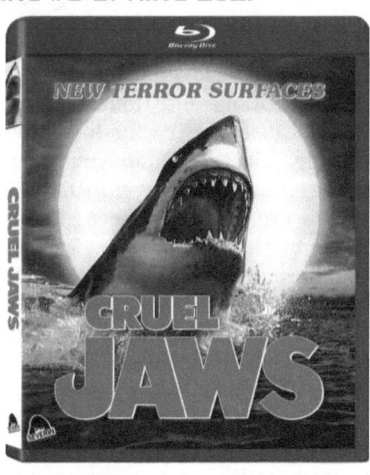

Banned since its release back in 1930, *Ingagi* has finally been unleashed on the public for the first time in 90 years! My interest in this film stems solely from an interest in *King Kong* (1933), which this film helped to inspire. Considering I was born 55 years after this film was released, I can't say that I enjoyed it. Not only is it pretty boring for someone in my age range, it's also naturally very politically incorrect. The film is Volume 8 of Kino Lorber's "Forbidden Fruit: The Golden Age of the Exploitation Picture", so if vintage banned films interest you as a film historian you might like it. The Blu-Ray comes with two commentaries, the first by series curator Bret Wood, and the second by film historian Kelly Robinson, who speaks in depth on ape-themed horror films. Full disclosure, I did not listen to both commentaries in full as that would mean watching *Ingagi* three times (I'm no sadist!), but, I did sample both commentaries and am pleased to say that both are very informative. They are not the type of commentators who run out of things to say and simply describe what's happening on screen, and are very well informed. I suggest watching *Ingagi* with the commentaries myself if you take the plunge.

This is another banned film for legal reasons (it used footage from *Jaws 2* illegally in addition to being a *Jaws* rip-off). Like *Ingagi*, I only watched it because of my interest in another film: *Jaws* (1975). Though titled *Cruel Jaws*, this film passed itself off as *Jaws 5* when it came out in 1995. It's what you would call a Frankenmovie in that it was cobbled together using shark footage from other movies, most notably *The Last Shark* (1981) and *Deep Blood* (1989). I watched this film on YouTube initially, as that was the only way I could find it. In 2015, Scream Factory planned to give it its first-ever Blu-ray release, but the illegal usage of pirated footage and music gave them cold feet. Now the film is available from Severin Films on Blu-Ray, and yes, the picture is a huge improvement over what I saw on YouTube and is very clear. So good quality all around, with special features and even an extended alternate version of the film! The standard Blu-Ray is still available, but I snagged a limited edition version with a "Jaws 5" cover and a novelization of the movie by Brad Carter! (Will I ever read it? Hell no! But's it's a great little collector's item.) If the limited edition tickles your fancy over the standard version, you might search eBay for it.

LOST LETTERS

Hi John! I've been wanting to tell you how much I've loved your books on un-made Kong and Godzilla films. THEN I discovered your incredible fanzine. THEN I found your page here on Facebook. I never DREAMED there were others out there so fascinated by the idea of unmade films, or alternative versions that might have been. I thought your books were a cool one off-thing, but your mag has blown me away.

The Lost Films Fanzine is my very favorite new magazine since *Video Watchdog*! I have bought and devoured the first two issues on Kindle; but I loved them so much I am going to pick up the paper copies, too. I am currently reading the third, but when I can I'll grab the physical version also. I'm also loving your daily posts here on Facebook; I've actually set my preferences to see your posts first on my feed.

Much like *Video Watchdog* was, *Lost Films* is like having a friend around that likes the same kind of thing you do. What IF King Kong had fought Ebirah? What if John Forbes-Robertson had replaced Christopher Lee as the new Hammer Dracula? Talk like that, where I live, would only get you oddball looks. I hope you know how much I appreciate your efforts! Keep up the great work, and hopefully we can talk more in the future. I wish I had something to contribute, but I'll gladly learn all I can from your great research. I hope your mag goes for a very long time!

My Best,

John Michael Seven

And I appreciate your feedback! It warms my heart to know that the 'zine is doing what it set out to do. And I'm glad that the 'zine's Facebook page also provides a nice distraction. If anyone else is interested in the FB page, it's "John LeMay's Lost Films". Thanks again for the words of encouragement John!

Thank you for running this page, John. It is fascinating and scholarly, on topics that I love. Facebook is such a depressing drag anymore, but your posts are always great and are a bright spot in my day. Thanks again. Belle Frost

Thank you Belle!!!

Happy New Year John! Just a fellow fan writing to show appreciation. Been reading your books for the last few years. Always fun reads and always look forward to your upcoming works.

I'm guessing you know director Tom Kotani passed away last month? Was wondering if you might do a piece on him for an upcoming issue of *The Lost Films Fanzine*? Particularly the four Rankin-Bass films he worked on. Since they are kinda rare (not necessarily lost). *Last Dinosaur* and *Bermuda Depths* are part of my childhood. Finally watched *Ivory Ape* recently. And saw *Bushido Blade* on YouTube not long ago. If not, maybe your friends at the Kaiju Transmissions Podcast could do an episode soon?

Either way, looking forward to the next *Movie Milestones*. Always wanna support a fellow monster fan (especially these days) and you got mine, sir! Take care! - Michael

Michael, thanks for the kind words and I too was saddened to hear of his passing and have sent your message along to KT (fingers crossed). I don't have any plans for articles on Kotani's works at the moment, but then again, he did almost do a Nessie movie back in the Seventies, so...

THE LOST FILMS FANZINE #5 SPRING 2021

THE BICEP BOOKS CATALOGUE

The following titles are available for purchase on Amazon.com, and are available to bookstores at a wholesale discount via Ingram Content Group (ISBNs of available editions listed for this purpose)

THE BIG BOOK OF JAPANESE GIANT MONSTER MOVIES SERIES

The third edition of the book that started it all! Reviews over 100 tokusatsu films between 1954 and 1988. All the Godzilla, Gamera, and Daimajin movies made during the Showa era are covered plus lesser known fare like *Invisible Man vs. The Human Fly* (1957) and *Conflagration* (1975). Softcover (380 pp/5.83" X 8.27") Suggested Retail: $19.99 SBN:978-1-7341546-4-1

This third edition reviews over 75 tokusatsu films between 1989 and 2019. All the Godzilla, Gamera, and Ultraman movies made during the Heisei era are covered plus independent films like *Reigo, King of the Sea Monsters* (2005), *Demeking, the Sea Monster* (2009) and *Attack of the Giant Teacher* (2019)! Softcover (260 pp/5.83" X 8.27") Suggested Retail: $19.99 ISBN: 978-1- 7347816-4-9

This second edition of the Rondo Award nominated book covers un-produced scripts like *Bride of Godzilla* (1955), partially shot movies like *Giant Horde Beast Nezura* (1963), and banned films like *Prophecies of Nostradamus* (1974), plus hundreds of other lost productions. Softcover/Hard-cover (470pp. /7 X 10") Suggested Retail: $24.99 (sc)/$39.95(hc)ISBN: 978-1-73 41546-0-3 (hc)

This sequel to *The Lost Films* covers the non-giant monster unmade movie scripts from Japan such as *Frankenstein vs. the Human Vapor* (1963), *After Japan Sinks* (1974-76), plus lost movies like *Fearful Attack of the Flying Saucers* (1956) and *Venus Flytrap* (1968). Hardcover (200 pp/5.83" X 8.27")/Softcover (216 pp/ 5.5" X 8.5") Suggested Retail: $9.99 (sc)/$24.99(hc) ISBN:978-1-7341546 -3-4 (hc)

This companion book to *The Lost Films* charts the development of all the prominent Japanese monster movies including discarded screenplays, story ideas, and deleted scenes. Also includes bios for writers like Shinichi Sekizawa, Niisan Takahashi and many others. Comprehensive script listing and appendices as well. Hardcover/Softcover (370 pp./ 6"X9") Suggested Retail: $16.95(sc)/$34.99(hc)ISBN: 978-1-7341546-5-8 (hc)

Examines the differences between the U.S. and Japanese versions of over 50 different tokusatsu films like *Gojira* (1954)/*Godzilla, King of the Monsters!* (1956), *Gamera* (1965)/ *Gammera, the Invincible* (1966), *Submersion of Japan* (1973)/*Tidal Wave* (1975), and, many, many more! Softcover (540 pp./ 6"X9") Suggested Retail: $22.99(sc) ISBN: 953221-77-3

This second volume examines the differences between the European and Japanese versions of tokusatsu films including the infamous "Cozzilla" colorized version of *Godzilla, King of the Monsters!* from 1977, plus rarities like *Terremoto 10 Grado*, the Italian cut of *Legend of Dinosaurs*. The book also examines the condensed Champion Matsuri edits of Toho's effects films. Coming 2022.

Throughout the 1960s and 1970s the Italian film industry cranked out over 600 "Spaghetti Westerns" and for every *Fistful of Dollars* were a dozen hilarious, some of them hilarious. Many of these lesser known Spaghettis are available in bargain bin DVD packs and stream for free online. If ever you've wondered which are worth your time and which aren't, this is the book for you. Softcover (160pp./5.06" X 7.8") Suggested Retail: $9.99

THE LOST FILMS FANZINE #5 SPRING 2021

THE BICEP BOOKS CATALOGUE

CLASSIC MONSTERS SERIES

Kong Unmade explores unproduced scripts like *King Kong vs. Frankenstein* (1958), unfinished films like *The Lost Island* (1934), and lost movies like *King Kong Appears in Edo* (1938). As a bonus, all the Kong rip-offs like *Konga* (1961) and *Queen Kong* (1976) are reviewed. Hardcover (350 pp/5.83" X 8.27")/Softcover (376 pp/ 5.5" X 8.5") Suggested Retail: $24.99 (hc)/$19.99(sc) ISBN: 978-1-7341546-2-7(hc)

Jaws Unmade explores unproduced scripts like *Jaws 3, People 0* (1979), abandoned ideas like a Quint prequel, and even aborted sequels to *Jaws* inspired movies like *Orca Part II*. As a bonus, all the Jaws rip-offs like *Grizzly* (1976) and *Tentacles* (1977) are reviewed. Hardcover (316 pp/5.83" X 8.27")/Softcover (340 pp/5.5" X 8.5") Suggested Retail: $29.99 (hc)/$17.95(sc) ISBN: 978-1-7344730-1-8

Classic Monsters Unmade covers lost and unmade films starring Dracula, Frankenstein, the Mummy and more monsters. Reviews unmade scripts like *The Return of Frankenstein* (1934) and *Wolf Man vs. Dracula* (1944). It also examines lost films of the silent era such as *The Werewolf* (1913) and *Drakula's Death* (1923). Softcover/ Hardcover(428pp/5.83"X8.27") Suggested Retail: $22.99(sc)/ $27.99(hc)ISBN:978-1- 953221- 85-8(hc)

Volume 2 explores the Hammer era and beyond, from unmade versions of *Brides of Dracula* (called *Disciple of Dracula*) to remakes of *Creature from the Black Lagoon*. Completely unmade films like *Kali: Devil Bride of Dracula* (1975) and *Godzilla vs. Frankenstein* (1964) are covered along with lost completed films like *Batman Fights Dracula* (1967) and *Black the Ripper* (1974). Coming Fall 2021.

NOSTALGIA

Written in the same spirit as *The Big Book of Japanese Giant Monster Movies*, this tome reviews all the classic Universal and Hammer horrors to star Dracula, Frankenstein, the Gillman and the rest along with obscure flicks like *The New Invisible Man* (1958), *Billy the Kid versus Dracula* (1966), *Blackenstein* (1973) and *Legend of the Werewolf* (1974). Coming 2021.

Written at an intermediate reading level for the kid in all of us, these picture books will take you back to your youth. In the spirit of the old Ian Thorne books are covered *Nabonga* (1944), *White Pongo* (1945) and more! Hardcover/Softcover (44 pp/7.5" X 9.25") Suggested Retail: $17.95(hc)/$9.99(sc) ISBN: 978- 1-7341546-9-6 (hc) 978- 1-7344730-5-6 (sc)

Written at an intermediate reading level for the kid in all of us, these picture books will take you back to your youth. In the spirit of the old Ian Thorne books are covered *The Lost World* (1925), *The Land That Time Forgot* (1975) and more! Hardcover/Softcover (44 pp/7.5" X 9.25") Suggested Retail: $17.95 (hc)/$9.99(sc) ISBN: 978-1-7344730 -6-3 (hc) 978- 1-7344730-7-0 (sc)

Written at an intermediate reading level for the kid in all of us, these picture books will take you back to your youth. In the spirit of the old Ian Thorne books are covered *Them!* (1954), *Empire of the Ants* (1977) and more! Hardcover/ Softcover (44 pp/7.5" X 9.25") Suggested Retail: $17.95(hc)/ $9.99(sc) ISBN: 978-1-7347816 -3-2 (hc) 978 -1-7347816-2-5 (sc)

THE LOST FILMS FANZINE #5 SPRING 2021

THE BICEP BOOKS CATALOGUE

CRYPTOZOOLOGY/COWBOYS & SAURIANS

Cowboys & Saurians: Prehistoric Beasts as Seen by the Pioneers explores dinosaur sightings from the pioneer period via real newspaper reports from the time. Well-known cases like the Tombstone Thunderbird are covered along with more obscure cases like the Crosswicks Monster and more. Softcover (357 pp/5.06" X 7.8") Suggested Retail: $19.95 ISBN: 978-1-7341546-1-0

Cowboys & Saurians: Ice Age zeroes in on snowbound saurians like the Ceratosaurus of the Arctic Circle and a Tyrannosaurus of the Tundra, as well as sightings of Ice Age megafauna like mammoths, glyptodonts, Sarkastodons and Saber-toothed tigers. Tales of a land that time forgot in the Arctic are also covered. Softcover (264 pp/5.06" X 7.8") Suggested Retail: $14.99 ISBN: 978-1-7341546-7-2

Southerners & Saurians takes the series formula of exploring newspaper accounts of monsters in the pioneer period with an eye to the Old South. In addition to dinosaurs are covered Lizardmen, Frogmen, giant leeches and mosquitoes, and the Dingocroc, which might be an alien rather than a prehistoric survivor. Softcover (202 pp/5.06" X 7.8") Suggested Retail: $13.99 ISBN: 978-1-7344730-4-9

Cowboys & Saurians: South of the Border explores the saurians of Central and South America, like the Patagonian Plesiosaurus that was really an Iemisch, plus tales of the Neo-Mylodon (a giant ground sloth), a menacing monster from underground called the Minhocao, Glyptodonts, shark-men and even a three-headed dinosaur! Coming Summer 2021 ISBN: 978-1-953221-73-5

UFOLOGY/THE REAL COWBOYS & ALIENS IN CONJUNCTION WITH ROSWELL BOOKS

The Real Cowboys and Aliens: Early American UFOs explores UFO sightings in the USA between the years 1800-1864. Stories of encounters sometimes involved famous figures in U.S. history such as Lewis and Clark, and Thomas Jefferson.Hardcover (242pp/6" X 9") Softcover (262 pp/5.06" X 7.8") Suggested Retail: $24.99 (hc)/$15.95(sc) ISBN: 978-1-7341546-8-9\(hc)/978-1-7344730-8-7(sc)

The second entry in the series, *Old West UFOs*, reports spanning the years 1865-1895. Includes tales of Men in Black, Reptilians, Spring-Heeled Jack, Sasquatch from space, and other alien beings, in addition to the UFOs and airships. Hardcover (276 pp/6" X 9") Softcover (308 pp/5.06" X 7.8") Suggested Retail: $29.95 (hc)/$17.95(sc) ISBN: 978-1-7344730-0-1 (hc)/ 978-1-7344730-2-5 (sc)

The third entry in the series, *The Coming of the Airships*, encompasses a short time frame with an incredibly high concentration of airship sightings between 1896-1899. The famous Aurora, Texas, UFO crash of 1897 is covered in depth along with many others. Hardcover (196 pp/6" X 9") Softcover (222 pp/5.06" X 7.8") Suggested Retail: $24.99 (hc)/$15.95(sc) ISBN: 978-1-7347816 -1-8 (hc)/978-1-7347816-0-1(sc)

Early 20th Century UFOs kicks off a new series that investigates UFO sightings of the early 1900s. Includes tales of UFOs sighted on the *Titanic* as it sunk, Nikola Tesla receiving messages from the stars, an alien being found encased in ice, and a possible virus from outer space!Hardcover (196 pp/6" X 9") Softcover (222 pp/5.06" X 7.8") Suggested Retail: $27.99 (hc)/$16.95(sc) ISBN: 978-1-7347816-1-8 (hc)/978-1-73478 16-0-1(sc).

65

BACK ISSUES

THE LOST FILMS FANZINE

ISSUE #1 SPRING 2020 The lost Italian cut of *Legend of Dinosaurs and Monster Birds* called *Terremoto 10 Grado*, plus *Bride of Dr. Phibes* script, *Good Luck! Godzilla*, the King Kong remake that became a car comm ercial, Bollywood's lost *Jaws* rip-off, Top Ten Best Fan Made Godzilla trailers plus an interview with Scott David Lister. 60 pages. Three variant covers/editions (premium color/basic color/ b&w)

ISSUE #2 SUMMER 2020 How 1935's *The Capture of Tarzan* became 1936's *Tarzan Escapes*, the Orca sequels that weren't, Baragon in Bollywood's *One Million B.C.*, unmade *Kolchak: The Night Stalker* movies, *The Norliss Tapes*, *Superman V: The New Movie*, why there were no *Curse of the Pink Panther* sequels, *Moonlight Mask: The Movie*. 64 pages. Two covers/ editions (basic color/b&w)

ISSUE #3 FALL 2020 Blob sequels both forgotten and unproduced, *Horror of Dracula* uncut, *Frankenstein Meets the Wolfman* and talks, myths of the lost *King Kong Spider-Pit* sequence debunked, the *Carnosaur* novel vs. the movies, *Terror in the Streets* 50th anniversary, *Bride of Godzilla* 55th Unniversary, Lee Powers sketchbook. 100 pages. Two covers/editions (basic color/b&w)

ISSUE #4 WINTER 2020/21 *Diamonds Are Forever's* first draft with Goldfinger, *Disciple of Dracula* into *Brides of Dracula*, *War of the Worlds That Weren't Part II*, *Day the Earth Stood Still II* by Ray Bradbury, *Deathwish 6*, *Atomic War Bride*, *What Am I Doing in the Middle of a Revolution?*, *Spring Dream in the Old Capital* and more. 70 pages. Two covers/editions (basic color/b&w)

MOVIE MILESTONES

ISSUE #1 AUGUST 2020 Debut issue celebrating 80 years of *One Million B.C.* (1940), and an early 55th Anniversary for *One Million Years B.C.* (1966). Abandoned ideas, casting changes, and deleted scenes are covered, plus, a mini-B.C. stock-footage filmography and much more! 54 pages. Three collectible covers/ editions (premium color/ basic color/b&w)

ISSUE #2 OCTOBER 2020 Celebrates the joint 50th Anniversaries of *When Dinosaurs Ruled the Earth* (1970) and *Creatures the World Forgot* (1971). Also includes looks at *Prehistoric Women* (1967), *When Women Had Tails* (1970), and *Caveman* (1981), plus unmade films like *When the World Cracked Open*. 72 pages. Three collectible covers/editions (premium color/basic color/b&w)

ISSUE #3 WINTER 2021 Japanese 'Panic Movies' like *The Last War* (1961), *Submersion of Japan* (1973), and *Bullet Train* (1975) are covered on like celebrated author Sakyo Komatsu's 90th birthday. The famous banned Toho film *Prophecies of Nostradamus* (1974) are also covered. 124 pages. Three collectible covers/ editions (premium color/ basic color/ b&w)

ISSUE #4 SPRING 2021 This issue celebrates the joint 60th Anniversaries of *Gorgo*, *Reptilicus* and *Konga* examining unmade sequels like *Reptilicus 2*, and other related lost projects like *Kuru Island* and *The Volcano Monsters*. Also explores the *Gorgo*, *Konga* and *Reptilicus* comic books from Charlton. 72 pages. Three collectible covers/editions (premium color/basic color/b&w)

www.ingramcontent.com/pod-product-compliance
Lightning Source LLC
Chambersburg PA
CBHW021431070526
44577CB00001B/163